"Over the past thre[...] Bootsma has proven t[...] [...] [...]ministry are in sync with the Holy Spirit, and I believe her new book is exactly what the Church needs to hear in this momentous hour in history!"

Dr. Ché Ahn, senior leader, Harvest Rock Church, Pasadena, CA; president, Harvest International Ministry; international chancellor, Wagner University

"*When Jesus Splits the Sky* is a very timely work by Patricia Bootsma. It brings the great hope of the Church before the largely unsuspecting Body of Christ. She offers ten practical actions that Christians can take to prepare their hearts and their futures for Jesus' imminent return. Learn how you can be spiritually prepared for the greatest event since the creation."

John Arnott, founder, Catch the Fire World

"For decades I've been blessed to witness Patricia's life as a consistent lover of Jesus and a passionate intercessor. Countless times she has stood with us in prayer when we needed it most. As we press forward with hope day by day until the Lord's return, friends like her are a vibrant source of comfort and wisdom along the way."

Dr. Heidi Baker, PhD, cofounder, Iris Global

"I believe the last generation of this age will be the greatest generation, equipped with abounding grace to overcome the increasing lawlessness. I'm confident *When Jesus Splits the*

Sky will function like a polished tool in the Potter's hand to promote that required greatness. Patricia is one of the Holy Spirit's purest vessels, and He will find great delight in using this book for His last-days purpose."

Kyle Hubbart, associate pastor and prayer room director, River in the Hills Church, Austin, TX

"*When Jesus Splits the Sky* is a rich and practical guide on how to keep the fire of our first love burning bright. Th testimonies and Patricia Bootsma's insights into Jewish culture are transformational. This book is solid food for hungry souls that long for a deeper encounter with their heavenly Bridegroom."

Dr. Arleen Westerhof, co–lead pastor, God's Embassy Amsterdam; codirector, European Prophetic Council

When

JESUS

SPLITS

the

SKY

When

JESUS
SPLITS
the
SKY

PREPARATION FOR HIS RETURN
AND OUR ETERNITY

PATRICIA BOOTSMA

Chosen

a division of Baker Publishing Group
Minneapolis, Minnesota

Published by Chosen Books
Minneapolis, Minnesota
ChosenBooks.com

Chosen Books is a division of
Baker Publishing Group, Grand Rapids, Michigan

Printed in the United States of America

Library of Congress Cataloging-in-Publication Data
Names: Bootsma, Patricia, 1965– author.
Title: When Jesus splits the sky : preparation for his return and our eternity / Patricia Bootsma.
Description: Minneapolis, Minnesota : Chosen Books, a division of Baker Publishing Group, [2025] | Includes bibliographical references.
Identifiers: LCCN 2024023254 | ISBN 9780800772772 (paperback) | ISBN 9780800773038 (casebound) | ISBN 9781493448784 (ebook)
Subjects: LCSH: Second Advent. | Future life.
Classification: LCC BT886.3 .B64 2025 | DDC 236/.9—dc23/eng/20240708
LC record available at https://lccn.loc.gov/2024023254

Cover design by InsideOut Creative Arts, Inc.

Baker Publishing Group publications use paper produced from sustainable forestry practices and postconsumer waste whenever possible.

25 26 27 28 29 30 31   7 6 5 4 3 2 1

This book is dedicated first of all to my heavenly Father: You forever changed my life with Your unconditional love. To Jesus—King, Bridegroom, and Judge: How I love Your appearing (2 Timothy 4:8)! And to Holy Spirit: Your presence is as necessary as oxygen.

I have been blessed to have an incredible family—John, my loving husband of 34 years; Judah, our amazing firstborn and only son; and five beautiful daughters—Gabrielle, Aquila, Phoebe, Zoe, and Glory Anna. Four of our children are married, and with their anointed spouses have given us the joy of nine adorable grandchildren.

Lastly I want to dedicate this book to my mom, Jean Boersma, who is 91 and who not only loves Jesus but often speaks of His return.

I am grateful for spiritual fathers and mothers who have helped me on this journey of life—John and Carol Arnott, Chester and Betsy Kylstra, Heather Johnston, and Cindy Jacobs. It is incredible to have people who believe in you and give you tools to help you go from "glory to glory."

CONTENTS

Foreword by Cindy Jacobs   11

Introduction   13

1. From Lukewarmness to Wholeheartedness   17

2. From Living without Margins to Sabbath Rest   33

3. From Ingratitude to the Power of Thankfulness   49

4. From Brokenness to Communion   63

5. From Pride to Humility   77

6. From Offense to Freedom   89

7. From Bitterness to Forgiveness   105

8. From Orphan Heart to Sonship   115

9. From Trials to Triumph   135

10. From This Life to the Next   147

Notes   169

FOREWORD

During the 1980s, I became aware that there were roots of pain and unforgiveness in my personal life that needed to be dealt with. If I had read this book then, it would have greatly accelerated my healing!

It is not easy to be as transparent as Patricia has been. She has targeted strongholds with deep insight that will penetrate lives in a loving and personal way. Out of her own challenges, she shares abiding truths that not only led to her own healing but now, through the power of the written word, will lead to the freedom of many others.

I love that she begins with what I consider to be the main thing—our wholehearted passion for the Lord. In the first chapter she reminds us of a very important and sometimes overlooked fact: Jesus is returning soon. We are to love Him and wait for His return while being fully engaged in occupying until He comes. I know I personally have regular checkups with the Father to see if I am on track and that my lamps are full for His return. In life's busyness, amid the current shakings going on all around us, this needs to be our focus: "Are we ready?"

Being passionate for Jesus is something Patricia understands. The words she writes are full of keys to help us lean into our relationship with God. Just as the natural world needs tending and gardens must be kept free from weeds, so does our heart as we go through regular struggles. I don't ever want to be lukewarm. This takes work on our side. I found myself "doing the work" while reading this book. It was a refreshing exercise for me, and it will be for you, too!

Her chapter on Sabbath rest challenged me anew as I fight for the Sabbath rest as a full-time traveling minister. I try to block days off in my travel schedule to rest. One personal way I keep it is to not go out shopping on Sundays except for necessities. This is not legalism, but a way for me to keep the Lord's day holy. Everyone might have that same conviction.

I tend to be a workaholic, and I need healthy biblical bounds. The Lord spoke to me one day and said, *"Cindy, your body is not a machine. Don't treat it like one!"* Ouch! I needed that!

An important reminder found in chapter 3 is the power of thanksgiving. There are times I have veered away from that as a practice. Can you believe there have been times when I did not thank the Lord for intervening on my behalf? It is embarrassing to admit. Patricia gives powerful examples of the beauty and power of being grateful.

Read each chapter carefully. The one on forgiveness opened up a need to pray over a current situation in my life. Dealing with bitter roots was one of the keys I learned in the 1980s to break strongholds.

Whether you are a new believer in following Christ or, like me, have been saved for over half a century, *When Jesus Splits the Sky* will change your life.

Cindy Jacobs, Generals International, Dallas, Texas

INTRODUCTION

Our citizenship is in heaven, from which we also eagerly
wait for the Savior, the Lord Jesus Christ.

Philippians 3:20

I t was an unremarkable prayer time years ago until the inner
voice of the Lord broke through my thoughts: *Patricia, how
is it I have made you a prophetic voice, but you have no idea of
the particulars of My coming again, the ultimate prophecy of all
time?* What could I say other than "Good point, God"?

That encounter and more like it rattled me enough to seek
out in Bible study, revelation, and heart impact the climax of
all human history when Jesus splits the sky.

Some 300 prophetic promises are recorded in the Old Testament that speak of Jesus' first coming. At least 150 chapters
speak of the transition from this age to the next, including His
Second Coming. As Jesus fulfilled all prophecies of His first
appearing, He will surely fulfill all pertaining to His coming
again.

The words of Haggai 2:6–9 are relevant to the days we are living in:

"For thus says the LORD of hosts: 'Once more (it is a little while) I will shake heaven and earth, the sea and dry land; and I will shake all nations, and they shall come to the Desire of All Nations, and I will fill this temple with glory,' says the LORD of hosts. 'The silver is Mine, and the gold is Mine,' says the LORD of hosts. 'The glory of this latter temple shall be greater than the former,' says the LORD of hosts. 'And in this place I will give peace,' says the LORD of hosts."

The shaking and groaning of wars, rumors of wars, famines, earthquakes, pandemics, persecution, the reaching of nearly all the unreached people groups, and more are intensifying like the labor pangs of a woman about to give birth. The "birth" is the Second Coming of Jesus and the transition of this age to the next (see Matthew 24; Romans 8:22). More and more people will seek out the "Desire of All Nations," who is Jesus Christ. The coming glory will be much greater than what we have thus far experienced.

The dichotomy of good and evil, light and darkness is echoed in Joel 2:11, "The day of the LORD is great and very terrible," and in Isaiah 60:1–2:

Arise, shine; for your light has come! And the glory of the LORD is risen upon you. For behold, the darkness shall cover the earth, and deep darkness the people; but the LORD will arise over you, and His glory will be seen upon you.

The greatest and the worst are coming. A worldwide awakening, a harvest of souls, and greater glory will coincide with darkness arising, the nations raging against the ways of the Lord (see Psalm 2), and "the beginning of sorrows" (Matthew 24:8).

Ultimately, for all who have ears to hear, what is coming is a wedding. The Father has promised His Son a Bride, the Church, and He is working to prepare her for that day. A pure, passionate, victorious Bride is emerging. "Let us be glad and rejoice and give Him glory, for the marriage of the Lamb has come, and His wife has made herself ready" (Revelation 19:7). To that end, this book was written. May we all be transformed to heed the healing and strengthening of our hearts and lives, so we will stand before Him on that day as a radiant Bride.

From the Scriptures, from my own life, and from the lives of many others, this book is about practical and inspired truths and stories to help us resist all that hinders us and live in fullness as we long for Jesus' return. Someday when we see Him face-to-face, every effort we have made to live for His glory will be well worth it. So let's stride into places of the heart to bring the living water made available through the sacrifice of Jesus. He wants to get what He paid for on the cross. He desires His Bride.

1

FROM LUKEWARMNESS TO WHOLEHEARTEDNESS

I don't want to just talk about the fire, be near the fire,
or think about how I once had the fire. I have to burn.

A spontaneous prophetic chorus in a prayer room

I have heard it said, "A Christian not interested in the return of Jesus is like a bride not interested in her wedding day. It's abnormal." The Holy Spirit longs to awaken our hearts in passion for Jesus. The hour is approaching when the King of kings, the Judge, the Bridegroom will split the sky.

And the primary focus of the return of Jesus is Jesus! The book of Revelation starts off by saying, "The Revelation of Jesus Christ." What Jesus did in revealing the Father through His first coming, the Father will do in revealing Jesus in His Second Coming. The Father greatly desires to speak to the nations about His Son. Every eye will see Him. Every knee will bow. And there will be mourning when He comes (see Revelation 1:7). Suddenly there will be no more ambiguity—Jesus is the Messiah. Those who dismissed Him as simply a historical figure, or even a lunatic or liar, will mourn, since they believed a lie and did not cultivate a heart of love for Him.

The Greatest Commandments

The Jewish rabbis state that Moses gave Israel 613 commandments. Jesus reduced these to two:

> "'You shall love the LORD your God with all your heart, with all your soul, and with all your mind.' This is the first and great commandment. And the second is like it: 'You shall love your neighbor as yourself.' On these two commandments hang all the Law and the Prophets."
>
> Matthew 22:37–40

Loving God, others, and ourselves is more important than everything recorded in the Bible about obeying commandments, living a moral life, and gaining wisdom. It is the heart that God is after, more than our works or service.

But it is one thing to know this, and another to have the revelation drop the nine inches from our heads to our hearts. When we wake up each morning, may we determine to grow in love during that day. And as we lay our heads on the pillow at night, may we ask for a heart for God that burns ever brighter, and dreams and revelations that enhance our love walk.

In His address to seven churches recorded in Revelation 2 and 3, the first and last churches were rebuked by Jesus for essentially the same thing.

Ephesus had lost her first love. Jesus said:

> "I have this against you, that you have left your first love. Remember therefore from where you have fallen; repent and do the first works, or else I will come to you quickly and remove your lampstand from its place—unless you repent."
>
> Revelation 2:4–5

And Jesus did not mince words to the Laodicean church for being lukewarm:

> "Because you are lukewarm, and neither cold nor hot, I will vomit you out of My mouth. Because you say, 'I am rich, have become wealthy, and have need of nothing'—and do not know that you are wretched, miserable, poor, blind, and naked—I counsel you to buy from Me gold refined in the fire, that you may be rich; and white garments, that you may be clothed, that the shame of your nakedness may not be revealed; and anoint your eyes with eye salve, that you may see."
>
> Revelation 3:16–18

Evidently the Laodiceans had status, wealth, and worldly accomplishments, yet they lacked what really mattered—what had eternal significance.

For both the Ephesians and the Laodiceans, and indeed for today's Church, Jesus' admonition is to repent, turn, and go after a first-love zeal, a hot heart. People often use the image of Jesus standing at the door and knocking—"Behold, I stand at the door and knock. If anyone hears My voice and opens the door, I will come in to him and dine with him, and he with Me" (Revelation 3:20)—in the context of salvation. Still, Jesus said it to a believing people who had lost their ability to draw close, to hear the voice of the Bridegroom, and to open the entirety of their hearts to His presence.

The Wedding to Come

Years ago I was awakened suddenly by a physical shaking in my home. My husband John, lying beside me, stayed asleep. It seemed to be mild earth tremors. Looking at the clock, I saw it was 2:22 a.m. Then I heard in my heart, *Matthew 22:2*. Not recognizing that Scripture reference, I lay in the dark, wondering what was happening.

A few minutes later it started again, a physical shaking as though the bed were moving around. Again I glanced at the clock. It was now 2:25 a.m., and these words came: *Matthew 22:5*.

I turned on a light and read those Scriptures. Matthew 22:2: "The kingdom of heaven is like a certain king who arranged a marriage for his son." Matthew 22:5: "But they made light of it and went their ways, one to his own farm, another to his business."

At that moment, in the early morning hours, I trembled under the weight of God's glory. I knew this was a clear message of the need to grasp the imperative truth that there is a celestial wedding to come, and that ignoring or making light of this fact amid the busyness of life is a grave error. I cried out to the Lord to reveal to me what it means that we are invited to the marriage supper of the Lamb.

The Church should be passionate for her Bridegroom, reflecting Jesus' message to the two churches in the book of Revelation—to stop being lukewarm and to return to our first love. How can we move from lukewarmness to wholehearted love for Jesus? And what does it mean that we are invited to the marriage supper of the Lamb?

We find a wedding theme all through the Bible. At least sixteen passages refer to God or Jesus as our Bridegroom.

Beginning in the Garden of Eden, the Lord created Adam and Eve to be "one flesh" (Genesis 2:24). He made them in His own image, longing for fellowship as He came to walk with them "in the cool of the day" (Genesis 3:8). On Mt. Sinai the Lord invited His people to be a "special treasure to Me above all people . . . a kingdom of priests and a holy nation" (Exodus 19:5–6). God said in Isaiah 62:5, "As a young man marries a virgin, so shall your sons marry you; and as the bridegroom rejoices over the bride, so shall your God rejoice over you."

John the Baptist called himself "the friend of the bridegroom" (John 3:29). Jesus alluded to Himself as "the bridegroom [who] will be taken away" (Matthew 9:15). Paul spoke of husbands and wives as a symbol of Christ and the Church: "Husbands, love your wives, just as Christ loved the church and gave Himself for her, that He might sanctify and cleanse her with the washing of water by the word, that He might present her to Himself a glorious church" (Ephesians 5:25–27).

The book of Revelation often speaks in wedding terminology. The word *revelation* itself means "apocalypse," which in turn means "unveiling." A bride in ancient Israel was veiled to the public, but when she and her groom came out of the wedding *chuppah* (chamber), the bridegroom unveiled her for the wedding feast and proudly put her on display for all to see.

In Revelation 19:7–9 a voice from God's throne said:

"Let us be glad and rejoice and give Him glory, for the marriage of the Lamb has come, and His wife has made herself ready." And to her it was granted to be arrayed in fine linen, clean and bright, for the fine linen is the righteous acts of the saints.

Then he said to me, "Write: 'Blessed are those who are called to the marriage supper of the Lamb!'"

Right after this wedding admonition, John in the book of Revelation saw Jesus coming on a white horse: "In righteousness He judges and makes war. His eyes were like a flame of fire, and on His head were many crowns" (Revelation 19:11).

The connection of these two passages shows the "wedding and the war," in which the Bridegroom is also a Judge who fiercely defends and rescues His Bride.

Revelation 21 speaks of the New Jerusalem coming out of heaven "as a bride adorned for her husband" (verse 2), and John heard a loud voice saying, "Behold, the tabernacle of God is with men, and He will dwell with them, and they shall be His people. God Himself will be with them and be their God" (verse 3).

These final chapters of the Bible urge us to leave behind lukewarmness and return to our first love for Jesus. He is our Bridegroom, the One who is coming to split the sky.

Ancient Jewish Weddings

If we do not understand Jewish customs and culture, we miss the deeper meaning of Bible teaching. In the Upper Room Discourse, Jesus was speaking to His disciples after celebrating Passover, before His death on the cross the next day:

"Let not your heart be troubled; you believe in God, believe also in Me. In My Father's house are many mansions; if it were not so, I would have told you. I go to prepare a place for you. And if I go and prepare a place for you, I will come again and receive you to Myself; that where I am, there you may be also."

John 14:1–3

Jesus was speaking in wedding language.

In New Testament times, Jewish weddings were initiated and arranged primarily by the father of the groom, but also by the parents of the bride. Jeremiah 29:6 says, "Take wives for your sons and give your daughters to husbands." Once the bride was chosen, the bridegroom would go to her parents' home and take four important things with him.

First, a skin of wine. If the parents agreed, the hopeful bridegroom would pour a cup of wine known as the cup of betrothal. If the bride accepted the proposal, she would indicate so by drinking the wine, making the engagement official. Second, money, called a *mohar* or bride price, was paid to the bride's parents to offset the loss of her labor in the home. Third, a marriage contract, called a *ketubah*, was signed to show that they were legally betrothed. Dissolving such an agreement, even though the marriage was not yet consummated, would require divorce papers to be signed. Last, the bridegroom would leave gifts for the bride as a pledge of his return.

It is noteworthy that the bride, from the day of her betrothal, was set apart and veiled when she went into public.

The bridegroom would then leave her and return to his father to build a bridal chamber onto his father's house. This was the place he was preparing to bring her for the second part of the wedding, the consummation. Once the chamber was built, the groom's father would inspect it to ensure that specifications were met. When the father was satisfied that all was in order, usually within a year, he would release his son to go and get his bride, even at midnight.

The bridegroom's friends would go with him in a procession to the bride's house, blowing shofars and proclaiming in the streets, "Behold, the bridegroom cometh." She had to be ready because she did not know exactly when he was coming. For this reason the bridegroom was called "a thief in the night," because he would come suddenly at an hour unknown to the bride. She had to be watching and living with the expectation that he could come at any minute.

The phrase Jesus used about His Second Coming—"of that day and hour no one knows" (Matthew 24:36)—describes when the bridegroom would go to claim his bride. Four men would carry the *palanquin* (carriage) on their shoulders to take the bride back to the groom's house. This was known as the *nissuin*, the "taking up" or "catching up" of the bride. Ten virgins carrying tall torches would accompany the bride to the bridal chamber.

At this point, the second part of the wedding, the consummation, was sealed with another cup of wine, appropriately called the "cup of consummation." The bride and groom would enter the bridal chamber (*chuppah*) for seven days to consummate the wedding. The friends of the bridegroom would stand at the door and announce when the bride and groom came out from the *chuppah* to the family and guests waiting for the wedding feast to begin.

There are many parallels between ancient Jewish weddings and Jesus as the Bridegroom with the Church as His Bride.

First, Jesus chose His Bride by the will of the Father: "You did not choose Me, but I chose you" (John 15:16).

Also, in the Upper Room on the night before His crucifixion, during the traditional Passover meal, Jesus initiated a betrothal ceremony. In the Jewish wedding, two cups of wine symbolize the two parts of the wedding—the first during the betrothal, and the second at the official wedding (and then the consummation). In the Passover there are four cups of wine, each representing one of the four expressions of deliverance promised by God in Exodus 6:6–7, and each accompanied by an "I will" statement: "I will bring out," "I will rescue," "I will redeem," and "I will take."

At His last Passover with His disciples, Jesus took the cup and said, "I will not drink of this fruit of the vine from now on until that day when I drink it new with you in My Father's kingdom" (Matthew 26:29). Why did He say that? Because the fourth cup of wine parallels the second cup of wine at a Jewish wedding in its call for consummation—or "I will take you as My Bride." Jesus was alluding to the fact that that fourth cup of wine, the cup of consummation, is partaken of in the bridal *chuppah*. That will occur in the wedding to come.

Jesus said He needed to go to the Father since He was going to prepare a place for us. He is indeed preparing a home, a *chuppah* or dwelling place, for us to be with Him forever. When will He come?

> "Of that day and hour no one knows, not even the angels in heaven, nor the Son, but only the Father. Take heed, watch and pray; for you do not know when the time is."
>
> Mark 13:32–33

Finally, the Bride price Jesus paid was His own life (see 1 Peter 1:18–19). And the gift Jesus left with us, His Bride, is the Holy Spirit: "He who has prepared us for this very thing is God, who also has given us the Spirit as a guarantee" (2 Corinthians 5:5).

The Oil of Intimacy

The Bible speaks in different places of fire as indicative of an offering to the Lord, or a light in the world. The fire on the altar in the Temple, which the priests were to keep burning, was not to go out (see Leviticus 6:9). And when Jesus called His followers the light of the world, He described a lamp with a burning flame to be put on display and shine as a way to "glorify your Father in heaven" (Matthew 5:14–16).

The seven churches in Revelation 2–3 were called "lampstands," or ministries of light in the world. Jesus admonished five of the seven churches to repent, warning them what would happen to them if they did not. For the first and last church (as we saw at the beginning of this chapter), those warnings included having her lampstand removed if she did not return to her first love (Ephesus) and being spit out of His mouth if she did not cease to be lukewarm, but become zealous (Laodicea). Hence, lampstands or lamps that carry fire, which is kept burning by oil, speak of our ministry—the light or fire of love in our hearts that is kept burning through the oil we carry. That oil, I believe, is indicative of our intimacy with the Lord.

A wedding parable Jesus told exhorts us to go from lukewarm to wholehearted in our devotion for Him.

The ten virgins of Matthew 25:1–13 were waiting for the bridegroom, yet five were wise and five foolish. How were the five foolish? They "took their lamps and took no oil with them" (verse 3). How were the five wise? They "took oil in their vessels with their lamps" (verse 4). For the foolish, the lamps of ministry, jobs, and life's duties took precedence over cultivating the oil of intimacy with God in the secret place of relationship.

For the wise, oil was listed first as a priority above the call of ministry.

When the midnight shout went out, "Behold, the bridegroom is coming; go out to meet him!" (verse 6), the five burning with an abundance of intimacy were ready. But they could not impart their oil of intimacy to the other five, just as someone cannot impart his or her personal journey of love with Jesus to another. It must be cultivated in the secret place of passion and prayer.

To the foolish, the Lord said, "I do not know you" (verse 12). That is a phrase no one would ever wish to hear from the One who holds eternity in His hand.

Our daughter Zoe married at the height of the pandemic, May 20, 2020. At first my husband, John, and I encouraged her to delay the wedding. After all, the number of guests would be down to twenty due to restrictions. Yet Zoe and Lucas were determined to stay with their original date and location.

As I attended their beautiful wedding, the Lord whispered to my heart, *Even in the midst of crisis and turmoil, the wedding will go on.* Zoe's focus was not on an invisible virus wreaking havoc on the world. Her focus was on her beloved Lucas and their wedding.

Similarly, during global shakings, crises, wars, and more, our focus on our beloved Bridegroom with a heart longing for Him is the ultimate expression of our readiness for the epic event of all time.

King David, the "man after God's own heart" whose side job was to be the king of Israel, personified this longing in Psalm 27:3–5:

Though an army may encamp against me, my heart shall not fear; though war may rise against me, in this I will be confident. One thing I have desired of the LORD, that will I seek: that I may dwell in the house of the LORD all the days of my life, to behold the beauty of the LORD, and to inquire in His temple. For in the time of trouble He shall hide me in His pavilion; in the secret place of His tabernacle He shall hide me; He shall set me high upon a rock.

David was able to lose himself in the beauty of God even in the midst of armies gathered against him. My friend Christie Eisner says, "Earth is preparing for war, but heaven is preparing for a wedding."

The Fire of Abiding

How do we, like King David, keep the fire of our passion for the Lord burning? How do we move from being lukewarm to being wholehearted?

Any fire, to keep burning, takes fuel and tending. We place logs on the fire and maintain a good draft of oxygenated air. If the flame dwindles to embers, it must be stoked, fanned, and given more flammable substances.

In the same way, keeping the fire of our passion for the Lord burning takes tending. Don't be surprised when you experience spiritual warfare over your intimacy with the Lord. Why? Because dark entities know that those with a burning passion for Jesus shine most brightly and help extinguish the darkness. As Heidi Baker, American missionary to Africa, says, "Lovers make better workers."

In cultivating the passion of my own heart, I have noticed that both subtractions and additions are needed.

The subtractions are issues of the heart that have wounded us and tried to derail us from intimacy with Jesus and our

God-given destiny. These wounds must be dealt with and removed by the power of the Holy Spirit, as they hinder our hearts from being tender before the Lord.

Then there are the additions—times of prayer, times in God's Word, hearing His voice, and simply being in His presence, placing our hearts next to the fire of His love, causing our own hearts to warm.

First John 4:19 says, "We love Him because He first loved us." Seeing, hearing, and experiencing how much Jesus loves us awakens our own love for Him.

How do we drink of this love? John 15:9 beautifully records Jesus' instructions for His disciples to abide in Him as a branch abides in the vine, enabling it to bear fruit: "As the Father loved Me, I also have loved you; abide in My love." In this one verse we find two truths and one command. God the Father loves the Son. Jesus loves us with the same scope and quality of the love the Father has for Him. And we are commanded to abide in the love of God for us.

We are also to obey Him, and our joy will be full (see verses 10–11). To abide in the massive ocean of God's love takes a lifetime to learn, with a daily commitment to prioritize this transformative walk.

Meditating on the Word of God is another key to learning to abide. In essence, His Word becomes a doorway for us to encounter the Author of the Word.

In John 5 Jesus rebuked the Pharisees for searching the Scriptures without knowing that "these are they which testify of Me. But you are not willing to come to Me that you may have life" (verses 39–40). He went on to point out that they did not have the love of God in them. They had missed the point of the Scriptures—to draw us into relationship and encounter with the One who inspired the words written therein.

Paul also spoke of the power of meditation:

> Do not neglect the gift that is in you, which was given to you
> by prophecy with the laying on of the hands of the eldership.
> Meditate on these things, give yourself entirely to them, that
> your progress may be evident to all.
>
> 1 Timothy 4:14–15

The Hebrew word for meditate is *hagah*, meaning to reflect and ponder aloud to oneself. In Hebrew thought, to meditate on the Scriptures is to repeat them quietly in a soft droning sound. Regular repetition of key Scriptures and prophetic words creates a womb for us to encounter the One who spoke these words and for them to be accomplished in our lives.

It is not the words we seek but the Lord Himself, even as Jesus said in John 5:39–40: "You search the Scriptures, for in them you think you have eternal life; and these are they which testify of Me. But you are not willing to come to Me that you may have life."

As we seek the Lord, we may abide, encounter, and come near to Him using the practices of prayer, meditation, and waiting on Him.

Wholehearted Success

Jeanne Guyon, a French mystic born in 1648, wrote in her classic work *Experiencing the Depths of Jesus Christ* that we behold the Lord through Scripture. She had learned the art of waiting silently in the presence of the Lord, as Isaiah

40:31 says: "Those who wait on the LORD shall renew their strength."

Nineteenth-century English preacher Charles Spurgeon wrote:

> I dare say you will think it a very easy thing to stand still, but it is one of the postures which a Christian soldier learns not without years of teaching. . . . It is one of the most difficult to learn under the Captain of our salvation. The Apostle seems to hint at this difficulty when he says, "Stand fast, and having done all, still stand."[1]

As I have sought to learn how to abide and encounter the heart of God, increasing my passion for Him, I have found that learning to be still is imperative. When distractions come, such as emails to send or things I must do, I write them in my journal to get to later. I want my mind stilled from the world's noise to focus on the nearness of God.

Meditate on whatever Scripture the Lord directs you to. I often start with John 15:9, and I read, write, sing, say, or pray the Scripture repeatedly until I feel drawn into a kind of "zone" with the Holy Spirit, sensing the nearness of His presence.

Oftentimes tears will start to trickle down my face as I sense in my heart of hearts a warmth, an embrace, a closeness of a very loving, intimate God. This, to me, is really living. I come alive in His presence. I know I was born for this—to know and be known by God.

One of the things I declare every day to the Lord Jesus and over myself is this:

> You feel about me as the Father feels about You. I am Your beloved. You delight in me. I lean on Your heart because I

love You. That is who I am and what I do. I commit to receive from Your heart by feeding on Your Word and abiding in Your presence. I long to know the secrets of Your heart. I am defined by my Father in heaven.

I know that, in contrast to the world's definition of success, God loves me and I am a lover of God, so I am a success. Out of this love springs forth fruitfulness.

I can honestly say that, at this stage of my life, my main objective is to grow in love. Should Jesus tarry and I leave this earth, I want inscribed on my tombstone, *She learned to love.* Since love for God and others is number one in the heart of God, I want it to be the main thing in my own pursuit.

Daily abiding in the Lord has caused my heart to become tenderized. And daily abiding in the Lord will help you, too, to go from lukewarm to wholehearted in your devotion to Jesus.

You will still struggle at times, but you will find worldly pursuits falling away. Your love for Jesus and for others will grow, and peace will reign in your heart. You will no longer need position or influence or the accolades of others. Remember the words of the gospel song, "The cross before me, the world behind me." And you will find yourself saying with the old hymn, "Give me Jesus."

PRAYER

Lord, help me to love You with all my heart, to cultivate the oil of intimacy, and to know You as my first love. Remove everything in me that hinders this love. Help me be Your Bride with a burning heart, ready for that day when I see You face-to-face.

2

FROM LIVING WITHOUT MARGINS TO SABBATH REST

Thou hast formed us for Thyself, and our hearts are restless till they find rest in Thee.

St. Augustine, *Confessions*

I t was when the world was thrown into chaos that I learned a valuable lesson about Sabbath rest. I wish I had lived in this discipline decades before, because it has changed my life.

In March 2020, due to the COVID-19 pandemic, I was forced to cancel many flights for international and domestic speaking engagements. But it was a silver lining in a dark time.

Initially I felt out of sorts and wondered how I would contribute to the family finances. Then I remembered the desire that had been growing inside me to spend less time on the go and more time with the Lord. And something began to stir in my heart and mind regarding the Sabbath. What was it all about, and was I missing the point God was trying to make by instituting Sabbath rest? As news feeds circulated about a devastating virus, my heart was drawn to tuck in under the shadow of the wings of the Almighty (see Psalm 17:8) and hear His voice more clearly.

A response also welled up in my heart to repent of pride, on my part and on the part of the Body of Christ—pride in how we exuded a lack of need for God to show up. This applied to our nation as well as our churches and ministries. We were just carrying on, leaning on giftings, programs, and traditional structures. Now it felt as if the Lord was allowing the whole world to stand at attention. It was time we gave Him the attention He deserved.

C. S. Lewis' words came to me at this time: "God whispers to us in our pleasures, speaks in our conscience, but shouts in our pain: it is His megaphone to rouse a deaf world."[1]

I found myself repeatedly returning to Haggai 2:6–9, in which God says:

> "Once more (it is a little while) I will shake heaven and earth, the sea and dry land; and I will shake all nations, and they shall come to the Desire of All Nations, and I will fill this temple with glory," says the Lord of hosts. "The silver is Mine, and the gold is Mine," says the Lord of hosts. "The glory of this latter temple shall be greater than the former," says the Lord of hosts. "And in this place I will give peace," says the Lord of hosts.

As I said in the introduction, the Lord is orchestrating a tremendous worldwide revival and awakening, bringing many into the revelation of Jesus as the Desire of All Nations. He is also providing financially for His people and pouring out greater glory than we have ever witnessed. And in all of this, He is imparting peace and rest.

A prophet named Bob Jones prophesied in 2009 about the decades to come. The 2020s, he said, would be a decade of learning the rest of God.[2] Who knew then that the world would be forced to abandon the usual speed of the rat race?

I began to study Hebrews 3–4 with renewed interest. There the Lord emphasizes the rest we are to enter, which has everything to do with faith, obedience, trust, and keeping the Sabbath. We are to "be diligent to enter that rest" (Hebrews 4:11). And Hebrews 3 speaks of the children of Israel who hardened their hearts when tested in the wilderness and did not heed the voice of God, and did not enter His rest or the Promised Land. "They could not enter in because of unbelief" (Hebrews 3:19).

A new quest arose in my heart to know what true rest is, how it is connected to the Sabbath, and why the Lord emphasized it for the decade of the 2020s.

Enemies of *Shalom*

The word for peace in Hebrew, *shalom*, means much more than the absence of agitation or discord. It means completeness, wholeness, health, welfare, safety, soundness, tranquility, prosperity, perfectness, fullness, rest, harmony, and prosperity. The root in the ancient Hebrew is *shalam*, meaning complete, perfect, and whole. This is the wholeness the entire human race seeks.

One morning I awoke surprised to hear the clear inner voice of the Lord: *I am declaring war on anxiety and depression in My people.*

In addition to observing how an invisible virus wreaked fear-filled havoc on multitudes, both in the Church and outside of it, and from children to those in the highest positions of government and business, I began to search out some staggering statistics.

In the United States, 240.7 million prescriptions were filled in 2018 for antidepressants and anti-anxiety medications.[3] The U.S. Centers for Disease Control and Prevention reports that in 2021, 48,183 Americans died by suicide, about one every eleven minutes.[4] Nearly one-third of adults in the U.S. in 2023 reported symptoms of anxiety and depression, around half of those young adults between the ages of 18 and 24; and by 2020 just over nine percent of American children had been diagnosed with anxiety problems.[5] According to psychologist Robert Leahy, "The average high school kid today has the same level of anxiety as the average psychiatric patient in the early 1950's."[6] And every year up to eleven percent of Americans experience a panic attack.[7]

Anxiety and depression are closely linked, as Proverbs 12:25 states: "Anxiety in the heart of man causes depression." The medications prescribed for anxiety are often the same as those for depression. Psalm 37:8 says, "Do not fret—it only causes harm." I have heard it said, "Anxiety is temporary atheism," as we lose sight of God.

What else steals rest and *shalom*?

Busyness

Someone once said, "If the devil can't make us bad, he will make us busy." Both sin and busyness can cut us off from connecting with God, others, and even our own souls.

According to a 2021 Gallup survey, the average American full-time employee works about 44 hours per week, while about 41 percent work 45 or more hours per week.[8] In addition, many fail to use up their allotted vacations, or else they take work with them while away, making America the "no-vacation nation." One study showed that the productivity of a person working more than fifty hours a week plummets; and working up to seventy hours a week accomplishes no more than working 55 hours.[9]

Accomplishments and accumulation have, to many, become twin gods, driving them to neglect the pursuit of relationships and, most importantly, a deep connection with God.

John Mark Comer's classic book *The Ruthless Elimination of Hurry* addresses the question "What do I need to do to be the me I want to be?" by quoting scholar Dallas Willard: "You must ruthlessly eliminate hurry from your life. Hurry is the great enemy of spiritual life in our day." Comer adds:

> To walk with Jesus is to walk with a slow, unhurried pace. Hurry is the death of prayer and only impedes and spoils our worth. It is not consistent with love.[10]

Technology

Technology is another enemy that steals rest and *shalom*.

The internet became available in homes in 1995, and is widely said to decrease IQ, concentration, and contemplation. By 2000 text messaging had become popular. Facebook and Twitter went public in 2006, which is about when Instagram and other social media platforms started unfolding. In 2007 the first iPhone was introduced.

A 2020 Netflix documentary, *The Social Dilemma*, reported that the average iPhone user touches his phone 2,617 times a day—and twice that for millennials. Tristan Harris and Sean

Parker, Silicon Valley tech insiders, came forward as whistle-blowers in the documentary to purport that everything on social media platforms is designed intentionally for distraction. Managing the scarce commodity of our attention span is called the "attention economy." Silicon Valley companies are after your attention by displaying advertisements that help make them trillions of dollars. Our attention span is dropping each year. In 2000, it was twelve seconds. Now it is not quite eight seconds.[11]

Forbes magazine reports that "the average American spends 68 minutes per day on the top five social media platforms, equaling almost five percent of their life, or 3.81 years."[12] *The Globe and Mail* says that smartphones are making us stupid, antisocial, and unhealthy—yet we cannot seem to put them down. Interacting with social media was designed to generate spurts of dopamine, a neurotransmitter released in the brain, which can become addictive.[13] Many of us are, in fact, in full-blown addiction, checking that last text, clicking on Instagram, and reading the email even before we go to the bathroom in the morning.

Philip Zimbardo, professor emeritus at Stanford University, conducted a study showing that by the age of 21, the average American guy spends ten thousand hours playing videogames. Noting this study, John Mark Comer comments:

> In ten thousand hours, you could master any craft, or become an expert in any field—from Sumerian archeology to Olympic water polo. You could get your bachelor's degree and your master's degree. You could memorize the New Testament.[14]

All these enemies of *shalom* we have been discussing—anxiety, depression, busyness, obsession with technology, and much more—demonstrate how the world has been living without margins. How do we move from all that to Sabbath rest?

What *Is* Sabbath Rest?

In the beginning, God created for six days, then took a day to rest. Later, when the children of Israel were freed from Egyptian slavery, where they had worked every day, the Lord instituted Sabbath rest as the fourth Commandment—the only spiritual discipline to make the Ten Commandments. This command, which God gave Moses, is grounded in the creation story:

> "Remember the Sabbath day, to keep it holy. Six days you shall labor and do all your work, but the seventh day is the Sabbath of the LORD your God. In it you shall do no work: you, nor your son, nor your daughter, nor your male servant, nor your female servant, nor your cattle, nor your stranger who is within your gates. For in six days the LORD made the heavens and the earth, the sea, and all that is in them, and rested the seventh day. Therefore the LORD blessed the Sabbath day and hallowed it."
>
> Exodus 20:8–11

In Deuteronomy 5:15 God grounds the command of Sabbath observance in the experience of the Israelites' exit from the Egyptian slavery:

> "Remember that you were a slave in the land of Egypt, and the LORD your God brought you out from there by a mighty hand and by an outstretched arm; therefore the LORD your God commanded you to keep the Sabbath day."

Why did the Lord command Israel to keep the Sabbath? This was the first generation in 430 years to come out of slavery and grow up in freedom. Enslaved people do not get a Sabbath. The Lord knew that the spirit under which they had labored in Egypt needed to be broken. The land of Egypt, under Pharaoh, was driven to accumulate and acquire. She built massive pyramids on the backs of slaves and even storage cities to contain what they had accumulated. Honoring the Sabbath is a resistance to that spirit.

Theologian Walter Brueggemann has this to say concerning God's ways, as opposed to the Egyptian system:

> Sabbath is . . . an alternative to the demanding, chattering, pervasive presence of advertising and its great liturgical claim of professional sports that devour all our "rest time." . . . I have come to think that the Fourth Commandment on Sabbath is the most difficult and most urgent of the commandments in our society because it summons us to intent and conduct that defies the most elemental requirements of a commodity-propelled society that specializes in control and entertainment, bread and circuses . . . along with anxiety and violence.[15]

Just Stop!

The root word for *Sabbath* is *shavat* or *shabat*, which means rest or cessation—to stop working, stop wanting, stop worrying. Just stop!

Honoring the Sabbath is one of the three components listed in Isaiah 58 as part of the fast God chooses in order for us to be heard on high. The other two components are helping the poor and stopping the negativity.

When the Lord started to convict me of not observing the Sabbath, I realized that although I had endeavored to take a day off each week, that day consisted of doing the laundry, getting caught up on emails, answering the dings on my cellphone, and running to the store to stock up on groceries. I was not ceasing activities.

As I cried out to the Lord for His heart for Sabbath rest, three things came to me to engage in: more time with the Lord, more time with family or friends, and more time in nature. This latter surprised me, but I recalled many believers saying that when they became Christians, the sky seemed bluer and the birds sang more sweetly. This also became true for me. There is something of the wonder of nature that is therapeutic. The Japanese call it "forest bathing" to walk in nature and experience soul rest.

When John and I, along with our daughter Glory Anna, who was seventeen at the time, began to honor Sabbath rest in early 2020, we shifted into a much better place. As of sundown on Fridays, we turned off our phones, closed our computers, and spent the next 24 hours resting, having lingering time with God, playing board games, taking hikes on forest paths, reading books, spending time with friends, and practicing rest.

It was a game-changer. My ability to hear God's voice increased. My ability to love increased. I stopped experiencing tension or feeling overwhelmed. A calm settled over our home. Glory Anna, the youngest of our six children, loved that Mom and Dad were not busy on their computers or other work-related activities and were completely available. I wished we had practiced the Sabbath this way for most of our child-rearing years.

Many of us are living without margins and are less creative, less focused, less observant, less intuitive, less patient, less kind, less persuasive, and less appealing. Our judgment is impaired, causing us to make poor decisions, and our efficiency plummets.

Jesus said, "The Sabbath was made for man, and not man for the Sabbath" (Mark 2:27). The Pharisees and religious leaders had slipped into legalism. Orthodox Jews today list 39 activities they must avoid during the Sabbath, including turning on a light switch, flushing a toilet, and driving a car.[16] Interestingly, Jesus performed many of His miracles on the Sabbath, enraging the religious leaders. Was that a message that the Sabbath was meant to bring healing to God's people?

Studies have shown that the happiest people on earth are the Seventh-day Adventists, who observe the Sabbath weekly on Saturdays. Ninety-three percent of Seventh-day Adventists in North America and the North Asia-Pacific report being happy.[17] Adventists live ten years longer, on average, than most Americans. Keeping the Sabbath over an average lifetime equals ten years.[18]

Are we measuring success in society by the wrong metrics? If we are basing our success on social status, bank account, the value of our house or car, social media likes, church size, book sales, or speaking invitations, we are missing the point of Jesus' standard. Matthew 22:37–40 records the Greatest Commandments: to love God with all our heart, soul, and mind, and to love others as we love ourselves. When the Sabbath is honored in God's way, love increases.

Studies show that as wealth goes up, happiness goes down. The happiest income in the U.S. is a household income of $75,000 per year. Incomes of more than that show a decrease in happiness. If you make $25,000 or more per year, you are in the top ten percent of the world's wealth. If you make $34,000 or more, you are in the top one percent.[19]

Pride causes us to push harder to work and accomplish. Essentially we are saying, "I can't obey God's directive to rest for a day. I need to work seven days a week to sustain the lifestyle I want or am accustomed to."

Keeping the Sabbath requires humility and dependence on God. We are laying aside work or advancement in order to be with God and the people He has put into our lives. In fact, people who honor the Sabbath live all seven days differently. They maintain a rest and trust in God that resides deep within.

Your peace will determine your pace.

The crazy thing John and I noticed from our first year of keeping the Sabbath is that our household income was the highest in our thirty-year marriage. How was that possible? I cannot quite wrap my mind around it. God did it.

Two more real-life examples:

Critics thought that David Green, founder of Hobby Lobby, a family-owned arts and crafts company, had lost his mind when he felt led by the Lord to close his stores on Sundays to honor the Sabbath. At that time Sunday was the busiest shopping day. Nevertheless Green honored God and closed his stores, state by state, on Sundays. Initially sales dipped slightly, but by 2023 they had climbed to $7.9 billion; and Hobby Lobby is one of America's largest private companies.[20]

Chick-Fil-A, informally known as Christian Chicken, is also closed on Sundays, yet in 2022, Chick-Fil-A was the leading quick service restaurant chain in the United States by sales per unit, reporting approximately $6.71 million in sales per unit—in six days instead of seven.[21]

Your Appointment with God

In Leviticus 23 God prescribed various feasts and observances, in the spring and in the fall. We will look at these in chapter 4.

The Jewish people have been keeping these appointments for millennia, often unaware that these feasts speak of Yeshua (Hebrew for *Jesus*). But in Leviticus 23:3, before the feasts are listed, the Lord commanded Sabbath observance:

> "Six days shall work be done, but the seventh day is a Sabbath of solemn rest, a holy convocation. You shall do no work on it; it is the Sabbath of the LORD in all your dwellings."

The word for *convocation* in Hebrew is *miqra,* meaning a sacred assembly or holy gathering. In English the term can imply rehearsal. Is it possible that the Sabbath is a rehearsal for what is to come? I think it is.

Let's look at three other kinds of Sabbath, in addition to the one-day-a-week Sabbath to which we usually refer.

Sabbath for the Land

First, there is "a sabbath of solemn rest for the land" every seventh year, as the Lord instituted in Leviticus 25:4. The Lord was so serious about the land resting once every seven years that the children of Israel suffered severe consequences for lack of obedience in this area.

In Leviticus 26:33–35 the Lord warned that disobedience would cause the children of Israel to be scattered among the nations, so that "the land shall rest and enjoy its sabbaths" (verse 34). This was no empty threat; that is precisely what happened. The southern kingdom of Judah was taken captive by Babylon in the year 586 BC for seventy years.

Why seventy years? Second Chronicles 36:20–21 explains what happened when the king of Babylon overran Jerusalem:

> Those who escaped from the sword he carried away to Babylon, where they became servants to him and his sons until the rule of the kingdom of Persia, to fulfill the word of the Lord by the mouth of Jeremiah, until the land had enjoyed her Sabbaths. As long as she lay desolate she kept Sabbath, to fulfill seventy years.

In other words, for 490 years the children of Israel had not kept the seventh-year land Sabbath, and now they were enslaved for seventy years, until the land enjoyed the equivalent of one year of rest for every seventh year of those 490 years.

The Year of Jubilee

Another kind of Sabbath is the one that occurs every fifty years—the Year of Jubilee (see Leviticus 25:8–17). In this year the land was to return to its previous rightful owner, so that those who possessed nothing and had to sell land for debts could become debt-free. Slaves were also to be set free. Jubilee was a year of liberty, consecration, and rest.

Jesus, in His first sermon, quoted Isaiah 61:1, declaring that the Messiah's anointing and divine commission enabled Him "to proclaim liberty to the captives" (Luke 4:18).

The Sabbath of the Millennium

Finally there is the Sabbath of the Millennium.

The earth was created in six days, and the Lord rested on the seventh day. 2 Peter 3:8 says, "Do not forget this one thing, that with the Lord one day is as a thousand years, and a thousand years as one day." As we look at human history from the timeline of the Bible, we are coming near the end of six millennia of human existence. I believe we are coming near to what is called the Sabbath of the Millennium, the thousand-year period after Jesus returns, spoken of in Revelation 20, when Satan is bound and the saints rule and reign with Christ.

As we keep the weekly Sabbath day, we are rehearsing or preparing for this millennial Sabbath, which we will enjoy in heaven with the Lord. After that time, Satan will be "cast into the lake of fire and brimstone" (Revelation 20:10). Then the New Jerusalem will come down out of heaven (see Revelation 21:2), and we will be with Jesus for eternity in glory.

Keep Your Appointment

God has special appointments with His people—in His feasts, on the Sabbath, and on the day of His return, as well as in the daily times we meet with Him. As the advice goes, usually attributed to Corrie ten Boom, "Have an appointment with the Lord and keep it."

One morning recently, as I sat down to spend time with the Lord, I heard Him speak to my heart. He said, *I am here; I showed up for My appointment with you.*

Wow! It never occurred to me that the God of the universe looks at my daily times with Him as an appointment that He Himself keeps.

Even as the Jewish people have been keeping appointments for years, possibly unaware that these all speak of Yeshua, God also has appointments with us, His people. He does not want us living without margins, scurrying around trying to get lots of things done instead of having a peaceful soul that trusts God enough to set apart one day for rest.

Will you make this appointment with God? Don't miss your appointments—your weekly Sabbath rest, your daily prayer life, and your eternal appointment to abide with Him forever.

— PRAYER —

Lord, forgive me for when I have been busy, distracted, and have not honored the Sabbath. I ask for Your grace to enter the place of rest. Help me abide in You and bear great fruit from that place of abiding.

3

FROM INGRATITUDE TO THE
POWER OF THANKFULNESS

*If I could impart anything to anyone through the laying
on of hands, I would impart an attitude of thanksgiving.*

Bill Johnson

Psalm 100:4 says, "Enter into His gates with thanksgiving, and into His courts with praise. Be thankful to Him and bless His name." When the Lord speaks of entering His gates with thanksgiving, He invites us into a rich and emotional inner journey that leads ultimately to entering the gates of heaven.

Is it possible that one cannot enter God's gates and courts without thanksgiving? The children of Israel discovered that those with a grumbling, complaining, unbelieving attitude could not enter the Promised Land. "The men whom Moses sent to spy out the land, who returned and made all the congregation complain against him by bringing a bad report of the land" (Numbers 14:36)—those ten spies died immediately by the plague.

The Bible mentions thankfulness 109 times. First Thessalonians 5:16–18 says, "Rejoice always, pray without ceasing, in everything give thanks; for this is the will of God in Christ Jesus for you." Can we give thanks in the midst of pain, trials, troubles, good times, triumphs, and tragedies?

A lifestyle of thankfulness is also referred to in Psalm 30:11–12 (NASB): "You have untied my sackcloth and encircled me with joy, that my soul may sing praise to You and not be silent. LORD my God, I will give thanks to You forever."

Thankfulness can be a sacrifice, as Psalm 116:17 says: "I will offer to You the sacrifice of thanksgiving, and will call upon the name of the LORD." But we don't always feel like being grateful.

Years ago John and I took our six children on a trip from Canada to Texas in our van. On the way home, embarking early one morning on the long journey home, we hit a dog that had run out in the road in front of us. That was bad enough. But immediately the van started sounding as though something significant was wrong.

Then the Lord spoke a directive into my mind. He said to give thanks and ask the children to join in singing thankful worship songs.

That was the last thing we felt like doing, but we obeyed. Instantly the atmosphere in the van shifted from one of fear and despair to hopefulness. And thirty minutes down the road, we discovered an automobile repair garage with a mechanic who fixed the van quickly and economically.

We knew that was a miracle—and a lesson. We have all remembered this lesson of how thankful worship changes circumstances.

When we ask, the Lord will somehow turn all events for our good. He promises this in Romans 8:28: "We know that all things work together for good to those who love God, to those who are the called according to His purpose." When He says *all things*, He means all. If our hearts stay right and our attitude pure, the Lord turns our mess into a message, and our tests into a testimony.

As the patriarch Joseph told his brothers, who had sold him into slavery, "You meant evil against me; but God meant it for good, in order to bring it about as it is this day, to save many people alive" (Genesis 50:20). In the pit and the dungeon, Joseph learned forgiveness and thankfulness, which helped promote him to second in command over all of Egypt and guide the land through seven years of famine.

Thankfulness causes growth and multiplication. In feeding the five thousand (see Matthew 14) and then the four thousand (see Matthew 15), Jesus took the loaves and the fish and gave thanks. Then they multiplied.

Thankfulness and Healing

When we are praying for someone to be healed of a physical infirmity, if that person gets better even ten percent, I have found that when we give thanks, the healing power very often will increase.

In the story of the healing of the ten lepers (see Luke 17:11–19), only one, a Samaritan, returned to give thanks to Jesus. That one who gave thanks received more than the others. Some translations quote Jesus as saying to him, "Your faith has saved you," referring to salvation and wholeness in addition to health.

We may be miffed when others get blessed instead of us. But if we can legitimately be happy for them, bless them, and be thankful that they were blessed, it helps release a blessing in our own lives.

I was surprised to hear a well-known revivalist pastor from California, Bill Johnson, say that if he could impart anything by the laying on of hands to anyone, he would choose to impart an attitude of thanksgiving. What? More than revival? Or the gift of healing or power encounters?

I worked as a registered nurse before becoming an ordained pastor at age thirty. All the staff observed that the patients with a positive, upbeat, thankful attitude were much more likely to recover quickly than those with a negative, complaining frame of mind.

Conscious Lifestyle magazine reports on something called the biology of gratitude—ways thankfulness is good for our bodies. Gratitude is good for our brains, activating the hypothalamus and producing dopamine, which helps us feel better and opens the door to many positive neurological effects. In a study called "Counting Blessings vs. Burdens," patients were instructed to keep a gratitude journal. Sixteen percent reported reduced symptoms, ten percent reported less pain; and subjects were far more motivated in their recovery.[1]

Other studies reveal that gratitude increases the quality of our sleep, decreases the time it takes us to fall asleep, and lengthens our sleep duration. This has a domino effect on the body, including boosting the immune system; decreasing systolic blood pressure and the stress hormone cortisol; and stabilizing the heart rate. Keeping a gratitude journal and sending thank-you notes decreases depression and anxiety. Gratitude yields increased energy, better self-esteem, increased productivity, improved job performance, improved likability, and increased happiness.[2]

Thankfulness blesses us physically, mentally, and emotionally, as we walk in obedience to the Lord by exercising this vital spiritual discipline.

Modeling Thankfulness

Thankfulness is something we can model to our children. Psalm 79:13 says, "We, Your people and sheep of Your pasture, will give You thanks forever; we will show forth Your praise to all generations." We can not only live in thankfulness but impart it to our children and all we come in contact with.

As I was leaving the birthing center with one of my newborn babies, the nurse called out, "Enjoy your baby." Something struck me at that moment. I was to enjoy parenting, of course, but also to be thankful for every stage in raising six kids, including the middle-of-the-night feedings, the multitudes of diapers changed, and the energy level it would take to keep up with the toddler years. And I was to model thanksgiving and praise—to this child and to each of my children.

With a heart of thanksgiving, there is no such thing as the "terrible twos." John and I renamed them the "terrific twos." Instead of dreading teenage rebellion, we declared, "We will not have one day of teenage rebellion. Our children are lovers of God." As of this writing, our youngest child has recently turned twenty, and this has been our experience.

Parents can model being thankful in prayer for the food about to be eaten, and ask their children to take opportunities to pray similarly. We can model thankfulness to the cook of the house, to the one who does the laundry, and to the one or ones who work hard to pay for the privilege of living in a home. We can encourage our children to be thankful to those who give birthday gifts, who open a door while they are walking into a store, or who give a compliment. A heart of thankfulness established in childhood will become a lifelong habit.

When we moved from Canada to the United States, we found that obtaining a driver's license for our youngest, Glory Anna, was not an easy process. It took months, as we navigated driver training for her as a homeschooled international student without a Social Security number, and obtained permission for her to take a driver's exam.

When Glory Anna was finally able to take the written test, she narrowly missed a passing grade. She was devastated. As she was crying and I was hugging her, I sensed the Lord telling me to ask her what she could be thankful for. We listed thanks that she had obtained the permission needed for driver's training, for the fact that she did so well there, and for how the Lord had led our steps in coming to America. The tears dried, and a new perspective emerged.

Initially we thought we had to wait months for a retest. Then we were told we needed to wait only seven days. Glory Anna triumphantly had her driver's permit at the end of the next week.

I heard a Christian leader share that he, his wife, and their small children had been living in an old, cold, run-down house early in his ministry. He asked his wife and children not to utter any words of complaint or negativity regarding their living situation. Sure enough, they were soon offered a spacious, beautiful home to live in by a wealthy friend, and from there the Lord used him to build a large Christian organization. He had learned the secret of positive confession and thankfulness.

Opportunities arise continuously for us to exercise gratitude, which opens the door to blessings.

Practicing Thankfulness

Seeing the glass of life as half full and not half empty shapes our level of contentment and joy.

Once John and I had a van with a small dent in one of the doors. I focused on that little dent each time I got into the van. One day the Lord rebuked me, clearly and lovingly, for focusing on the small dent and missing the gift of a reliable, functional van big enough for us and all our children. I repented for my attitude and began to thank the Lord for the van, and I no longer noticed the little dent.

The same principle can apply to relationships. One time, looking at my husband, I focused on the nose hairs that seemed to sprout after he turned forty. Yes, getting rid of nose hairs was good, but somehow I was missing his handsomeness, beautiful blue eyes, and, more importantly, his strong character and love for God, me, and our children.

It is better to major on the majors and minor on the minors. It is crazy how arguments can escalate over the smallest, most insignificant things. Marriage therapist Dr. John Gottman says, "The number one thing that couples fight about is exactly that: nothing." Bitter fights can ensue about what to eat for dinner, about misplaced keys, or about what is going out on garbage day. Gottman asserts that a "positive perspective" on the relationship is needed to buffer against negativity. In other words, be thankful.[3]

If you have experienced a failed marriage, can you be thankful for the children from that relationship or for lessons learned? In the death of a loved one, can you be grateful for the love you shared and the reality of heaven? When a job is lost, can you practice thankfulness for the experience gained while praying for a new opportunity?

One effective practice to promote thankfulness is keeping a thanksgiving journal. Writing short snippets of items or experiences to be thankful for enables us to slow down and appreciate all the good in life and the goodness of God. The old adage "Stop and smell the roses" helps us appreciate the little things we miss in a busy, high-speed lifestyle. Thankfulness for the way the sun rises over the trees, the dew on a leaf, the neighbor who keeps his lawn beautiful, the phone call from an old friend that sparks laughter, the money to purchase groceries, the gift of sight, the energy to exercise, the ability to turn on a faucet and clear water comes out. All these are not to be taken for granted.

On a mission trip years ago with a group of fellow Canadians, I spent three weeks in the Philippines, eating mostly beans and rice. The next leg of the journey brought me to Hong Kong, and I was never so happy to see a McDonald's and eat a hamburger. Then we went on to China, smuggling Bibles to distribute to the underground church, whose members were risking their lives to obtain them. I suddenly became aware that I had taken for granted my ability to own five Bibles that were not used nearly as much as they should. I determined at that time to become a woman of the Word.

Practicing thankfulness can include writing thank you notes, sending emails, or making phone calls to express gratitude. Bestselling author Sarah Ban Breathnach says, "Gratitude bestows reverence, allowing us to encounter everyday epiphanies, those transcendent moments of awe that change forever how we experience life and the world."[4]

Honoring Parents

I spent years of my life seeking inner healing, breaking off generational curses, forgiving my father, getting free of the pain of hurt, renouncing vows, and adjusting my life to be more Christlike. But somewhere in the good of healing, I forgot to see all the good in my family heritage.

The set of lenses through which I saw my younger life was tainted with negativity—what was not right, what I did not have, who had wronged me, and all I needed to be healed of. Simply put, I had a victim mentality. Yes, I was getting healed of the hurts in my heart, but I could not enter into honor and the joy of a relationship with my family of origin until I learned to be thankful for them.

The fifth Commandment is the only one with a promise attached:

> "Honor your father and your mother, as the LORD your God has commanded you, that your days may be long, and that it may be well with you in the land which the LORD your God is giving you."
>
> Deuteronomy 5:16

In 2003 our family moved back to my hometown of Stratford, Ontario, Canada, to pastor the church where John and I had met. My father's initial reaction was not necessarily welcoming: "Don't be expecting your mother to babysit those six kids of yours." I assured him I would not be asking for a family babysitting service.

Then the Lord began to speak to me about honoring my parents—my dad in particular. At first I assured the Lord that I *was* honoring him as I showed up at Christmas and sent him a Father's Day card. The Lord countered to my heart that it was not good enough, and He instructed me that I was to honor my father in ways that would speak to his heart. In particular, I was to sit in the coffee shop with my parents a few times a week. I assured the Lord that I had too many important things to do! But evidently the Lord felt this was important, as His insistent nudges for me to obey would not abate.

So I began to go to the coffee shop regularly to hear Dad tell war stories. He had grown up in the Nazi-occupied Netherlands during World War II. Listening to his stories gave me a new appreciation for where he and Mom had come from. I realized they were incredibly resilient—in the face of the Great Depression and a world war. They had each immigrated to Canada alone on a weeks-long transatlantic passage to come to a nation with no job opportunities and whose language they did not know.

Dad eventually became the largest dairy farmer in southwestern Ontario and a very successful real estate broker. I began to see how much I had learned from him in leadership, ingenuity, and people skills. And I loved growing up on the large farms he owned. He had bought me ponies and horses, and I had spent a lot of time riding in the open fields with the wind whipping through my hair. The hours I spent working in the barn taught me how not to be idle, and Dad paid me for my work from age fourteen until I left home.

My mother was (and still is) an incredibly hard worker. Everyone has a love language they predominantly express, and I began to see that Mom's love language was acts of service. She tirelessly cooked incredible meals, mended my torn jeans, cleaned my bedsheets, and kept an impeccable home.

Instead of despising my heritage, I began to see that the Dutch have a strong work ethic. They know how to stretch a dollar. The Dutch are tall and physically active, as they are often biking, walking, or skating. The Dutch tell you like it is, and you are never left wondering how they feel.

As I began to embrace greater thankfulness for my parents and heritage, a much greater level of love in my heart was released to them, and we enjoyed a closer relationship. (I will talk more about forgiving my father in chapter 8.) Eight years later, when my family moved away from Stratford, Dad, who had been less than welcoming when we came, wept as he said, "Do you have to leave?"

Recently I read the book *Twice Adopted* by Michael Reagan. The adopted son of Ronald Reagan and his first wife, actress Jane Wyman, had grown up with anger toward his biological birth mother, who had given him up for adoption. He wondered, *Why did she hate me so much to give me up? Why didn't she want me? What is wrong with me?* Only much later, after he became a believer, adopted for the second time by God, did he realize the sacrifice his unmarried teenage mother had made to ensure that he lived and went into a loving home. She did love him. She knew it was best that he went to a home with two parents who could provide for him. He became thankful for his birth mother, and this turned his life around.

Obedience to the fifth Commandment to honor your father and mother is sure to release the promise contained therein—that you will live long on the earth and that it will go well with you. Honoring and being thankful are two sides of the same coin. Let's be grateful for the families we were born into, no matter their flaws.

Thanksgiving in Eternity

The Bible contains numerous references to expressions of thanksgiving and honor in heaven. Revelation 7:12 says, "Amen! Blessing and glory and wisdom, thanksgiving and honor and power and might, be to our God forever and ever. Amen."

And look at this glimpse of the heavenly reality going on right now:

> [The four living creatures] do not rest day or night, saying: "Holy, holy, holy, Lord God Almighty, who was and is and is to come!" Whenever the living creatures give glory and honor and thanks to Him who sits on the throne, who lives forever and ever, the twenty-four elders fall down before Him who sits on the throne and worship Him who lives forever and ever, and cast their crowns before the throne, saying, "You are worthy, O Lord, to receive glory and honor and power; for You created all things, and by Your will they exist and were created."
>
> Revelation 4:8–11

There is a clear, overwhelming expression of thanksgiving and honor in heaven. It behooves us to gain a heart of gratitude now toward the Lord and toward others He has put into our lives. In the light of eternity, will some of the things we are tempted to grumble about really matter?

May we shine as lights, thankful people practicing and modeling what is happening in heavenly realms right now, and helping to usher heaven to earth.

--------------------- PRAYER ---------------------

Lord, thank You for Your love and goodness toward me. Help me recognize the many blessings You have provided, and to live with a grateful heart.

4

FROM BROKENNESS
TO COMMUNION

Eucharisteó—thanksgiving—always precedes the miracle.
Ann Voskamp, *One Thousand Gifts*

T he Eucharist is the celebration of the Lord's Supper or
Communion. The night before Jesus went to the cross,
He celebrated the Passover meal, otherwise known as
the Last Supper, with His disciples:

The Lord Jesus on the same night in which He was betrayed
took bread; and when He had given thanks, He broke it and
said, "Take, eat; this is My body which is broken for you; do
this in remembrance of Me." In the same manner He also took
the cup after supper, saying, "This cup is the new covenant in
My blood. This do, as often as you drink it, in remembrance

of Me." For as often as you eat this bread and drink this cup, you proclaim the Lord's death till He comes.

1 Corinthians 11:23–26

Communion, properly and regularly exercised, is an act of celebration of what Jesus accomplished on the cross. We declare to ourselves, to the Lord, and to the demonic realm that we believe in and apply the power of the blood of Jesus to every aspect of our lives, and we will continue to do this as we look to His return—in Paul's words, we will "proclaim the Lord's death till He comes." Ultimately, Communion is all about Jesus' return and getting ready for that day through what was accomplished through the broken body and shed blood of Jesus.

Since Jesus instituted Communion during the Passover meal, let's look back to the time of Moses, when the Lord instituted Passover, among other feasts, connecting His divine plan with the life of His Son.

Rehearsing for Jesus' Return

In Leviticus 23:1–2, just before commanding Sabbath observance (which we discussed in chapter 2), the Lord directed Moses to tell the people, "The feasts of the LORD, which you shall proclaim to be holy convocations, these are My feasts." God went on to describe the feasts the Hebrew people were instructed to observe.

One Hebrew word translated "feast" is *mo'ed*, meaning fixed time, appointment, appointed season, festival, feast, solemn assembly, or appointed place. First used in Genesis 1:14, the word *mo'ed* refers to God's creation of the sun, moon, and stars as "signs [signals] and seasons [*mo'ed*], and for days and years." The feasts are God's scheduled appointments He made with His people.

The word for *convocation* in Hebrew (as we noted in chapter 2) is *miqra*, meaning a sacred assembly or holy gathering. In English the term implies rehearsal. The feasts have past, present, and future fulfillments. In fact, God's entire plan of redemption is revealed in the progression of seven feasts or mileposts that unfold yearly in the Hebrew calendar.

Is it possible that the feasts the Lord describes in Leviticus 23, which the Jews have been practicing for more than 3,500 years, are rehearsals that speak of a greater truth? I believe they are.

Colossians 2:16–17 calls the feasts "a shadow of things to come, but the substance is of Christ." Wow! All the festivals and convocations listed in Leviticus 23—which we will look at in this chapter—have spoken of Yeshua (Jesus) all along. And every one of the major events in Jesus' life occurred during one of Israel's feasts.

Four of these feasts come in the spring: Passover, the Feast of Unleavened Bread, the Feast of Firstfruits, and the Feast of Weeks; and three come in the fall: the Feast of Trumpets, the Day of Atonement, and the Feast of Tabernacles. All the spring feasts were fulfilled in Jesus' first coming and the outpouring of the Holy Spirit at Pentecost, and all the fall feasts point to His Second Coming.

The Spring Feasts

The spring feasts speak of Jesus' first coming.

Jesus died on **Passover** on the fourteenth day of Abib, at the very time when the Passover Lamb was sacrificed: 3 p.m.

He became the Passover Lamb who through the atonement forever paid the price for our sin.

On the evening of the first Passover, God told the Hebrew people leaving Egypt not to allow their bread to rise with leaven, but to leave Egypt in haste. Passover celebrates God's miraculous deliverance of Israel from Egypt, after the angel of death in the tenth plague killed each of the firstborn of Egypt, but passed over every Hebrew home, where they had applied blood to their doorposts. The Lord instructed His people to commemorate this feast by getting all yeast out of the house for seven days. The yeast represented sin and was to be removed as a form of spiritual cleansing. The only type of bread eaten during Passover is matzo, bread made without yeast.

The next day, Abib 15, is the **Feast of Unleavened Bread**, with leaven symbolic of sin. Unleavened bread lasts longer and does not quickly go moldy. During the Feast of Unleavened Bread, sinless Jesus was buried, and His body never saw decay when He was in the tomb.

Jesus was raised from the dead on the third day, at the time of the **Feast of Firstfruits**, the sixteenth day of Abib. He is the "firstborn from the dead" (Revelation 1:5).

The **Feast of Weeks** or **Shavuot** occurs fifty days after the Feast of Firstfruits. Agriculturally it speaks of the wheat harvest in Israel. Biblically it commemorates the day God gave Moses and the children of Israel the Torah on Mount Sinai after seven weeks in the wilderness. This holiday also ends the fifty days of the counting of the omer between Passover and Shavuot.

Let me explain what that means. Beginning with the Sabbath of the Passover, God commanded the Israelites to bring the first measure (*omer* in Hebrew) of the early barley harvest to the priest as a thank offering for the upcoming harvest and a dedication to the Lord. Barley was considered a less significant harvest than the wheat harvest, which would begin around Shavuot.

According to Jewish tradition, there is deep meaning to the fifty days of counting the omer and reciting the prayer "Blessed are You, Lord our God, King of the universe, who has sanctified us with His commandments and commanded us to count the omer. Today is day one [or two, etc.]." This set-apart time marked the spiritual progression from Passover to Shavuot.

Shavuot occurred on the day also known as Pentecost (derived from the Greek word meaning "fiftieth"). After Jesus was raised from the dead on the Feast of Firstfruits, He appeared first to Mary at the tomb, then to His disciples, and to more than five hundred people at once, over forty days (see 1 Corinthians 15:4–6). Jesus told the believers to tarry in Jerusalem and pray, which they did in the Upper Room. Ten days later the Holy Spirit was poured out on the Day of Pentecost, at the exact time of Shavuot and fifty days after the Feast of Firstfruits.

The Fall Feasts

The fall feasts speak of the day when Jesus comes again.

The **Feast of Trumpets** or **Rosh Hashanah** falls on the first day of the seventh month (Tishri), which on the Hebrew calendar is a new moon. Thus the exact day and hour to begin are based on the first sighting of the sliver of the new moon. When the first sighting occurs, the Hebrew people were to celebrate by blowing shofars, or trumpets, to prepare the people to begin the feast. Various Bible references speak of Jesus coming again at the sound of the trumpet, the last trumpet, or the seventh trumpet (see Matthew 24:30–31; 1 Corinthians 15:51–52; 1 Thessalonians 4:16–17; and Revelation 11:15).

The ten days following the Feast of Trumpets are the Ten Days of Awe, or days of personal reflection, prayer, mourning, and repentance of sin. The **Day of Atonement** occurs on Tishri 10, also known as **Yom Kippur**, the holiest day of the year, when fasting is mandated and the high priest entered the Holy of Holies to make atonement for the sins of the people. It is also known as Judgment Day, when all will stand before Jesus face-to-face. Thankfully, for those who embrace His redemptive work on the cross, our deserved judgment fell on Him. He made atonement for us.

Lastly, the **Feast of Tabernacles** or **Sukkoth** begins on Tishri 15, a weeklong time of remembering when the Hebrew people lived in a *sukkah* or temporary booth after they left Egypt, as a sign of when God led them through the wilderness. This speaks of the time mentioned in Revelation 21:3: "Behold, the tabernacle of God is with men, and He will dwell with them, and they shall be His people. God Himself will be with them and be their God." Someday we will tabernacle or dwell with the Lord forever.

Unto a Wedding

In the first chapter we spoke of returning to our first love for Jesus, our Bridegroom, the One who is coming to split the sky. We also looked at the wedding language Jesus used in His last Passover, the Last Supper. And we noted that at the Last Supper, Jesus did not drink of the fourth Passover cup, saying, "I will not drink of this fruit of the vine from now on until that day when I drink it new with you in My Father's kingdom"

(Matthew 26:29). He is awaiting drinking the fourth cup, the cup of consummation, until His Bride is with Him eternally.

My friend Christie Eisner is married to a Jewish man. After she and John both came to faith in Yeshua, they still sought to honor John's parents by observing the Jewish holidays and celebrations. This began a 48-year study of the feasts of the Lord in Leviticus 23, in which Christie received incredible biblical and Holy Spirit revelation. She elaborates on the spring feasts in her first book, *Finding the Afikoman*, and on the fall feasts in her book *Watching and Waiting*.

Christie has this to say about the last Passover when Jesus was instituting Communion:

> He said, "Do this in remembrance of Me." What are we to remember every time we do Communion? That we are legally betrothed, and right now, we have a Bridegroom in heaven who is interceding for His bride and preparing a place to take us when He returns! He paid the bride price (mohar) with His blood, and then at the next Spring feast of Shavuot (Pentecost), He left a gift for His bride: the indwelling Holy Spirit!
>
> Hebrews 12:2 says, "that for the joy set before Him He endured the cross." What was that joy? It was us! He saw beyond the cross, the payment to "buy us back," and saw that day when He would finally have the reward of six thousand years of suffering since the enemy stole His bride in the garden.
>
> This is not a fairy tale. This is real, and we get to be part of it. So we can partake of this cup together, remembering what He remembers: "the love of our betrothal when we went after Him in the wilderness" (Jeremiah 2:2). Every Passover and every time we take Communion, we can lift our cup and say "yes" to Him again![1]

As Communion is ultimately about Jesus' return, it is also part of our preparation for His return, and our participation with a "Yes!" in our hearts to the Father's divine plan of the wedding to come for His Son.

Eucharisteó

Author and blogger Ann Voskamp and I have a lot in common. We are both Dutch-heritage Canadian authors who grew up on farms, married Dutch-heritage men, and home-schooled our six children. (She later adopted one more.) At one time we lived three kilometers from each other in southwestern Ontario. But now Ann is a four-time *New York Times* bestselling author!

Her first book, *One Thousand Gifts: A Dare to Live Fully Right Where You Are*, is one of the best books I have ever read. With her mystic, unusual writing style, Ann weaves her personal story in with deep biblical insights.

As a child, Ann and her family witnessed the tragic death of her younger sister under the wheels of a delivery truck in their farm driveway. The grief caused her mother to be hospitalized for a time in a mental health ward and her father to have a crisis of faith. Ann herself became anxious, depressed, and suicidal. Yet her life was forever changed by the revelation of *eucharisteó* and the keeping of a journal of one thousand things she was thankful for.

That word *eucharisteó* means "to be grateful." During the Last Supper Jesus gave thanks for the bread and wine. The Greek word for gave thanks in each of the four gospels comes from the root word *eucharisteó*, meaning "to be grateful." This word envelops the words *charis*, meaning "grace," and *chara*, meaning "joy." Grace, thanksgiving, joy. In short, *eucharisteó*—giving thanks—has the power to change lives through a "threefold cord" (Ecclesiastes 4:12) of the grace to express thanksgiving and find joy.

Voskamp writes:

> *Eucharisteo* means "to give thanks," and *give* is a verb, something that we do. God calls me *to do* thanks. *To give the thanks away.* That thanks-*giving* might literally become thanks-*living*. That our lives become the very blessings we have received. . . . *Eucharisteo* precedes the miracle. . . . God *gives* gifts and I *give* thanks and I unwrap the gift given: *joy*.[2]

Anxiety, depression, and fear melt in the revelation of a great God who gives us the grace to find thankfulness in all things, and that unleashes joy.

Voskamp further writes:

> The practice of giving thanks . . . *eucharisteo* . . . this is the way we practice the presence of God, stay present to His presence, and it is always a practice of the eyes. We don't have to change what we see. Only the way we see.[3]

Communion, taken rightly, points to the return of our Bridegroom King, which cannot be separated from thanksgiving.

Beni and Bill Johnson point out in their book *The Power of Communion* that it was amid Jesus' ultimate betrayal at the Last Supper that He gave an offering of thanksgiving:

> An impartation of thankfulness would have the greatest impact on the hearts and minds of people. It would literally change the world as we know it. Thankful people attract breakthrough.[4]

The Meal That Heals

John and I have taken Communion together nearly daily for more than a decade. As a result, we have been blessed in many ways and have experienced fewer colds, cases of flu, and other maladies in our home.

I remember reading many years ago about a man who took Communion every day and started to look younger, even passing through an international border at which the border guard could not believe he was as old as he was. That piqued my interest in taking Communion more than once a month at church.

But it is important that we not receive Communion in an unworthy manner. The apostle Paul makes a connection between sickness and partaking in Communion with active, willful sin in our lives:

> Whoever eats this bread or drinks this cup of the Lord in an unworthy manner will be guilty of the body and blood of the Lord. But let a man examine himself, and so let him eat of the bread and drink of the cup. For he who eats and drinks in an unworthy manner eats and drinks judgment to himself, not discerning the Lord's body.
>
> 1 Corinthians 11:27–29

When we partake of Communion, we are receiving a representation of the body and blood of Jesus that has value, that can redeem us or, without proper application, bring us judgment. The point is not to reduce Communion to a mindless ritual but to examine our hearts truthfully and repent of all forms of sin, including unforgiveness, grudges, bitterness, and any other vices that the Holy Spirit reveals.

Beni and Bill Johnson write that every time we take Communion, we remember what Jesus accomplished on the cross; we remind the devil of his failure; we align ourselves with our true identity; we release healing in spirit, soul, and body; we align ourselves with God; we repeat the testimony that Jesus died for us to be free of sin, sorrow, and sickness; and we testify to the radical, enormous love of God. Communion is a powerful tool of intercession.[5] It is also, according to Beni and Bill Johnson, an act of war:

> The Lord has given us basically four different weapons for spiritual warfare: the blood of Jesus (Communion), the Word of God, the name of Jesus, and praise. Those are the four basic weapons that we believers use in our life that defeat and overcome the assaults that the enemy brings against us. None of them are focused on the devil. All of them are focused on the provision of the Lord and the Person of the Lord Jesus Christ.[6]

Communion has been called the "meal that heals." Jessica Koulianos, wife of pastor and author Michael Koulianos, recounts a powerful testimony about her maternal grandfather, Roy Harthern.

Harthern, pastor of a large Assemblies of God church near Orlando, Florida, was dying of kidney cancer. A pastor friend and great Bible teacher began teaching Roy about the power of taking Communion every day. Harthern began to align himself daily with the body and blood of Christ through Communion.

One night the Lord Jesus Christ appeared to Roy in his hospital room and told him He was going to heal him. Subsequent tests showed that every trace of cancer was gone from

Roy's body, and that he now had the kidneys of a much younger man. His atheist doctor came to faith, and Harthern went on to live another twenty years, "sharing his testimony of God's healing and the power of Communion."[7]

Looking Back to Go Forward

The apostle Paul spoke of Christian marriage as a representation of Christ and the Church. Husbands are to love their wives "just as Christ also loved the church and gave Himself for her, that He might sanctify and cleanse her" (Ephesians 5:25–26), a glorious Bride without spot or wrinkle. Husbands are to give themselves sacrificially to their wives, while wives are to respect and submit to their husbands. Paul added, "This is a great mystery, but I speak concerning Christ and the church" (verse 32).

Just as marriage speaks of a greater reality, so does the act of participating in Communion. Paul was quoting Jesus:

> "This cup is the new covenant in My blood. This do, as often as you drink it, in remembrance of Me." For as often as you eat this bread and drink this cup, you proclaim the Lord's death till He comes.
>
> 1 Corinthians 11:25–26

As we participate in Communion regularly, we are looking back to the price Jesus paid on the cross as the Bride price for our redemption, to cleanse us from anything that separates us from Him in His holiness. We are also looking forward to the day Jesus comes again and ushers us to the wedding banquet where we will tabernacle with Him forever.

So let's take the bread and the cup together. Take it alone, or take it with your spouse, with your children, or with others around you. The Bible does not specify that you may take Communion only at church with a pastor. I strongly encourage taking Communion every day.

Let's give thanks and, like Jesus, see the incredible supernatural power of God unleashed in our lives. Let's look for and long for the fulfillment of entering into the ultimate Communion—the return of our Bridegroom King. Let's prepare for His return and our eternity. Let's say yes!

--- PRAYER ---

Jesus, thank You for dying for me so that I may live and receive all the benefits of life in You. Remind me to take Communion regularly as I proclaim what You accomplished on the cross, until You come again.

5

FROM PRIDE TO HUMILITY

Pride must die in you, or nothing of heaven can live in you.

Andrew Murray

Pride . . . is the complete anti-God state of mind. . . . As long as you are proud, you cannot know God. A proud man is always looking down on things and people, and, of course, as long as you are looking down, you cannot see something that is above you.

C. S. Lewis, *Mere Christianity*

The Bible has much to say about the tug-of-war between pride and humility. Derivatives of the word *pride* are mentioned in Scripture 125 times, and *humble* or *humility* is spoken of 84 times. Pride, as we will see, can cost one's destiny, including a home in heaven.

The nature of pride is insidious and difficult to detect in ourselves, as we are often blinded to its operation. Pride can cause us to feel as if we are the star in the constellation around which others need to revolve. It can mean we view ourselves as of higher importance, giving us unrealistic expectations of others to fit into our own preferred narrative. Our demands must be met; we view others' dreams as of lesser consequence; and we apply a double standard.

The proud can feel they are above the rules. They love to have access that others do not enjoy. They detest waiting in line. Pride projects an air of self-reliance and independence. The proud prefer (or need) to drive a slick car, wear the coolest clothes, and sit in VIP seats. Ordinary is not in their vocabulary; standing out is their style. Be seen, be heard, be strong, and for goodness' sake don't waste my time. Excellence, standards, deadlines, and productivity—all must be met above the feelings of others.

Where there is pride, there are problems. Proverbs 28:25 says, "He who is of a proud heart stirs up strife, but he who trusts in the LORD will be prospered." The proud lead a path of destruction in emotional hurt, atmospheric tension, anxiety, discouragement, and many other problems. Pride has broken many marriages. It has cost relationships with friends and led to estrangement and loneliness. James 4:6 and 1 Peter 5:5 both say, "God resists the proud, but gives grace to the humble." If there is anything we should not want to happen in our lives, it is to have God opposing us. Pride repels God's blessing.

In the Old Testament, Saul started as one who saw himself small in the tribe of Benjamin (see 1 Samuel 10:21–22). But after being anointed king of Israel, he felt he was above the rules for sacrificing the burnt offering, which was the responsibility of the prophet Samuel. It would result in the loss of his kingdom (see 1 Samuel 13:8–14). Later Saul did not follow through on God's directive to eliminate the Amalekites, preferring his own idea of saving the king and the best of the spoil. His disobedience caused God to reject him as king (see 1 Samuel 15). Saul's jealousy over David's military success led to his persecution of the one deemed his most loyal and valuable human asset. As a result Saul was defeated by the Philistines, costing his life, the lives of three of his sons, and many of his military men (see 1 Samuel 31).

God brings down the proud, as Proverbs 16:18 states: "Pride goes before destruction, and a haughty spirit before a fall."

King Nebuchadnezzar of Babylon was so proud that he had a giant golden statue created in his image, demanding that all bow down and worship it as soon as they heard the sound of music. He also walked about his royal palace and proclaimed, "Is not this great Babylon, that I have built for a royal dwelling by my mighty power and for the honor of my majesty?" (Daniel 3:30).

These words were still on his lips when the Lord declared from heaven that the kingdom would be taken from Nebuchadnezzar and that he would live "with the beasts of the field ... [and] eat grass like the oxen" until he recognized "that the Most High rules in the kingdom of men, and gives it to whomever He chooses" (Daniel 4:31–32).

Those words were fulfilled "that very hour" (verse 33) as the king became insane, behaved like an animal, and was driven out of society. But by the mercy of God, after a period of time, the king was restored and proclaimed,

"Now I, Nebuchadnezzar, praise and extol and honor the King of heaven, all of whose works are truth, and His ways justice. And those who walk in pride He is able to put down."

Daniel 4:37

The Unsinkable Ship

John and I took a transatlantic cruise from New York to Southampton, England, on Cunard's *Queen Mary 2* some years ago. A storm began to rage early in the voyage, causing wind gusts and waves greater than thirty feet in height. Many on the ship were struggling with seasickness, including me. Crew members said they had never seen a storm of this magnitude. They also said something disconcerting: We were over the area of the Atlantic Ocean where the RMS *Titanic* had sunk on April 15, 1912. Additionally, the captain of the *Queen Mary 2* bore a remarkable resemblance to photographs of Captain Edward Smith of the ill-fated ship.

Upon entering service, the *Titanic* was the largest and most luxurious ocean liner ever built. Named after the Titans of Greek mythology, it boasted hundreds of opulent first-class cabins, upscale restaurants, a gymnasium, a swimming pool, a Turkish bath, and many other commodities unknown in that era. Yet on her maiden voyage, the ship struck an iceberg and took just two hours and forty minutes to sink, with the loss of more than fifteen hundred lives.

The *Titanic* was not destroyed by an iceberg alone. It is widely believed that it sank due to arrogance.

One of the employees of the White Star Line, which operated the *Titanic*, was overheard declaring at the launch of this great vessel, "Not even God Himself could sink this ship!"

Many shared that view. Further, the ship was equipped with only twenty lifeboats (which actually surpassed the safety standards of the time) capable of holding 1,178 people, only about half of the 2,224 on board.

Throughout the day of April 14, 1912, the *Titanic* received warnings from other ships of drifting ice in the area. Captain Smith changed her route slightly but continued to steam ahead at nearly full speed. Late that evening, the lookout spotted an iceberg immediately ahead and alerted the bridge, but it was too late to prevent a collision.

The crew was poorly trained on how to evacuate the ship, and many of the lifeboats lowered into the ocean were only half full, with room for almost five hundred more people available.

The wireless operator of RMS *Carpathia*, one of the ships that had warned the *Titanic* of icebergs, received and responded to the *Titanic's* distress signal. Captain Arthur Rostron navigated 67 miles of perilous icefields in three and a half hours to rescue 706 survivors, transporting them to New York. He later received awards and was knighted. One of his crew described him like this:

> He was a believer in the power of prayer. When he was on the bridge, and everything went smoothly, I saw him stand a little to one side, close his eyes, and lift his uniform cap two or three inches above his head while his lips moved in silent prayer. [1]

Some have noted the contrast between the two captains of the *Titanic* and *Carpathia*. One steamed self-assuredly through a treacherous icefield, and the other was said to have prayed fervently as he navigated the icy waters to rescue survivors. Dare we say that one went down in history as proud and the other humble?

It seems worthy of note that in June 2023, an OceanGate submersible called *Titan* was on a dive to view the *Titanic's* remains almost two and a half miles below the ocean's surface. Sometime during the plunge, it imploded, killing all five onboard. Investigations are ongoing as of this writing, yet the disaster did not come as a complete surprise. Warnings given over five years noted design flaws of the submersible, with complaints issued to the U.S. government and Ocean-Gate leaders. All were ignored. Called by some an accident waiting to happen, the disaster occurred in the very location where lessons of history were unheeded and repeated 111 years later.

No Pride in Heaven

Several passages of Scripture speak of the demise of Lucifer, a glorious angelic being who fell from the heavenly domain. One of these is Isaiah 14:12: "How you are fallen from heaven, O Lucifer, son of the morning! How you are cut down to the ground, you who weakened the nations!"

Isaiah 14:13–14 goes on to record five "I will" statements by Satan. Each of these exposes the stronghold of pride:

> "For you have said in your heart: 'I will ascend into heaven, I will exalt my throne above the stars of God; I will also sit on the mount of the congregation on the farthest sides of the north; I will ascend above the heights of the clouds, I will be like the Most High.'"

The Lord responds to Lucifer's five pompous declarations with His own five judgments, which begin:

"You shall be brought down to Sheol, to the lowest depths of the Pit. Those who see you will gaze at you, and consider you, saying: 'Is this the man who made the earth tremble, who shook kingdoms, who made the world as a wilderness and destroyed its cities, who did not open the house of his prisoners?'"

Isaiah 14:15–17

Another prophetic passage is Ezekiel 28, addressed to "the king of Tyre." Many Church Fathers and contemporary leaders believe this passage speaks not just to the natural king of Tyre but to Satan himself:

"You were the seal of perfection, full of wisdom and perfect in beauty. You were in Eden, the garden of God; every precious stone was your covering: The sardius, topaz, and diamond, beryl, onyx and jasper, sapphire, turquoise, and emerald with gold. The workmanship of your timbrels and pipes was prepared for you on the day you were created.

"You were the anointed cherub who covers; I established you. You were on the holy mountain of God; you walked back and forth in the midst of fiery stones. You were perfect in your ways from the day you were created, till iniquity was found in you. . . .

"Your heart was lifted up because of your beauty; you corrupted your wisdom for the sake of your splendor; I cast you to the ground, I laid you before kings, that they might gaze at you. You defiled your sanctuaries by the multitude of your iniquities, by the iniquity of your trading; therefore I brought fire from your midst; it devoured you, and I turned you to ashes upon the earth in the sight of all who saw you. All who knew you among the peoples are astonished at you; you have become a horror and shall be no more forever."

verses 12–15, 17–19

Consider that Satan wanted to be like God, leading to his demise. One-third of the angels went with him.

The way of Jesus, by contrast, is that of the Suffering Servant, embracing children, touching and healing lepers, washing the disciples' feet, and embracing a cruel cross.

May we take seriously the insidious and demonic nature of pride and seek to rid our lives of this evil.

Dangerous Prayer

Here is a dangerous prayer: "Lord, reveal and deal with any pride in me." If we mean it, the Lord will orchestrate events to reveal threads or strongholds of pride He seeks to demolish.

David prayed similarly: "Search me, O God, and know my heart; try me, and know my anxieties; and see if there is any wicked way in me, and lead me in the way everlasting" (Psalm 139:23–24).

Andrew Murray defines humility as dependence on God:

Humility is perfect quietness of heart. It is to expect nothing, to wonder at nothing that is done to me, to feel nothing done against me. It is to be at rest when nobody praises me, and when I am blamed or despised. It is to have a blessed home in the Lord, where I can go in and shut the door, and kneel to my Father in secret, and am at peace as in a deep sea of calmness, when all around and above is trouble."[2]

There is a place in the heart of God where we can be immune to the trap of pride. It has everything to do with receiving our sense of worth and affirmation from the Lord Himself.

Jesus called out the proud religious leaders, who did not do this, when He said to them:

"I do not receive honor from men. But I know you, that you do not have the love of God in you. I have come in My Father's name, and you do not receive Me; if another comes in his own name, him you will receive. How can you believe, who receive honor from one another, and do not seek the honor that comes from the only God?"

John 5:41–44

Because these leaders did not know the love of God in their hearts, they sought the "fillers" of accolades from others, fillers like special seats in the synagogue or the praises of their fellow Jews.

Later, hanging on the cross, Jesus quoted David from Psalm 31:5: "Into Your hand I commit my spirit." Jesus' trust in His Father to redeem Him was so deep that He could offer up His life. Jesus knew that entering into weakness in the womb of a virgin and submitting to a Roman cross would not keep Him from the destiny the Father had for Him. In fact, it would fulfill it.

For us followers of Jesus, this passage says, "Lord, I belong to You. Therefore, this issue is not my problem; it is Yours. I will not engage in reactive self-defense but seek to forgive, keep my heart right, and trust You to turn this situation out for good."

This is an act of humility. This is knowing that the Lord fights for those who wait for and rely on Him. Instead of trying to take matters into our own hands, defend ourselves, and seek to preserve our reputation, we can lean back into His everlasting arms of love and confidently relinquish our "right to be right," trusting that time will tell where victory lines are drawn.

I never thought of myself as having a problem with pride until the Lord orchestrated a time when all my props for feeling good about myself were removed. I went from traversing the nations as an elite airline member, appearing on large platforms, cohosting a TV program, and rubbing shoulders with some of the who's who of the Christian world, to being called to start a house of prayer in a small church in the city close to where I grew up. While I was worshiping the Lord with a handful of musicians and intercessors, He spoke a question to my heart: *Patricia, am I enough for you?*

With tears streaming down my face, I answered, "Lord, You are enough for me. And if You want me to sit before You, worshiping and interceding for the rest of my life, that's okay."

A powerful shift occurred in my life at that time. Instead of drinking in the praises of people, I sought more to know how to live before the eyes of the One who was my endless source of love and honor. It did not matter so much what people thought of me. The criticisms did not sting so much. I appreciated the praises but no longer needed them. I felt more at peace and rest, and stopped striving for accomplishments to please people.

I encourage you to pray that dangerous prayer—at the beginning of this section and at the end of this chapter: "Lord, reveal and deal with any pride in me."

Generational Pride

I mentioned in chapter 3 that my parents immigrated to Canada from the Netherlands, and that the Lord led me into greater thankfulness for my parents and my Dutch heritage.

I was born in Canada but consider myself very much of Dutch stock. I am tall with blond hair and green eyes, love Gouda cheese, and even wore wooden shoes as a child. I have also, at times, vacillated from feeling insecure to being proud.

One day the Lord nudged me to repent of some of the negatives of my Dutch heritage.

There is a saying in Holland that goes like this: "God made the world, but the Dutch made Holland." The reasoning behind this saying is that the Netherlands—one of the three Low Countries—obtained more functional land from the sea by building dikes to hold back the water. For example, Amsterdam's Schiphol Airport lies at the bottom of what was once Haarlemmermeer Lake, more than sixteen feet below sea level. On the flip side, since *Netherlands* means "low-lying country," I have noticed small thinking and self-doubt in many Dutch I know, including myself.

But something shifted in my life after identificational repentance of pride and low (or small) thinking. I was freed of a generational trap I had stepped into, often unwittingly.

There is wisdom in reflecting on whether we have opened a door to pride for our generational heritage. We may have pride in our family name, our genetic or physical features, the stature our father held in the community, the house we grew up in, the car we were driven around in, the schools we attended. On the flip side, we may bear shame for all the factors just listed.

Either way, the heart of the Father is that we are free of pride, shame, or both.

When I am tempted to feel prideful, I reflect on Philippians 2:5–11:

> Let this mind be in you which was also in Christ Jesus, who, being in the form of God, did not consider it robbery to be equal with God, but made Himself of no reputation, taking the form of a bondservant, and coming in the likeness of men. And being found in appearance as a man, He humbled

Himself and became obedient to the point of death, even the death of the cross. Therefore God also has highly exalted Him and given Him the name which is above every name, that at the name of Jesus every knee should bow, of those in heaven, and of those on earth, and of those under the earth, and that every tongue should confess that Jesus Christ is Lord, to the glory of God the Father.

What an incredible Savior—to humble Himself to leave the glories of heavenly splendor to embrace humanity and to die on our behalf. May that kind of humility be reflected in us.

 PRAYER

Lord, reveal and deal with any pride in me. And I pray Psalm 36:11: "Let not the foot of pride come against me, and let not the hand of the wicked drive me away."

6

FROM OFFENSE TO FREEDOM

... that you may be sincere and without offense till the
day of Christ.

Philippians 1:10

Melissa and her sister did not speak for two years due
to a strained phone argument, which she felt later
concerned a topic of no consequence.

Hope felt perpetually demeaned by comments from her
sister, leading to fourteen years of no communication, ending
only with a fatal cancer diagnosis.

Christine and her brother did not speak for years because
instead of flying home for her daughter's baptism, he flew to
Las Vegas for a weekend of partying.

The names, reasons, and details vary, but all can be traced
to the nasty spirit of offense.

A growing trend within interpersonal relationships, families, and society at large points to an increase in what is known as offense. The United States leads the world in the number of lawsuits per person. U.S. business liability costs totaled $347 billion in 2021.[1] The rise of lawsuits has become serious business. Most of these are rooted in some sort of offense.

Families suffer when members refuse to speak to one another for extended periods due to some infraction committed years prior, the cause of which is often long forgotten. Forty percent of the participants in one U.S. study had experienced family estrangement.[2]

In the United States, the two largest political parties are so at odds that most members of Congress vote along party lines instead of working cohesively. Offense by a particular politician or party seems to fuel decisions to attempt to oust that individual or censure that party rather than work across the aisle or seek the good of the country.

The Rise of Offense

With heightened sensitivities and the rise of political correctness, many walk on eggshells, trying not to offend. We experience the censoring of free speech by seeing it labeled "hate speech" in order to attack religious freedom. Who has not noticed the recent trend of no longer saying "Merry Christmas" in favor of the more culturally acceptable "Happy holidays"? (After all, Christmas has the name *Christ* in it!) And one does not assume that a person's companion is a husband or wife but merely a "partner," as the couple may not be married.

An American university president offended a segment of his college community when a picture was posted of him wearing a sombrero at a costume party. He subsequently apologized.[3] A Yale University faculty member chose to resign after sparking protests when she said students should be able to wear whatever they want for Halloween costumes. She wrote in an email to students:

> American universities were once a safe space not only for maturation but also for a certain regressive, or even transgressive, experience; increasingly, it seems, they have become places of censure and prohibition.[4]

Woke is a slang term that describes someone alert to injustice in society, especially discrimination or racism. In itself that sounds innocent. Yet today's progressives have utilized "wokeism" as a worldview, undermining the foundations of the Christian faith. Today's woke movement and "cancel culture"—in which a person or organization seen as speaking or acting unacceptably is fired, ostracized, or boycotted, often with the help of social media—act against "offenses" committed by those who hold differing views from what is deemed acceptable. "Acceptable" does not include many biblical values.

The Black Lives Matter organization skyrocketed to prominence after the death of George Floyd, a black American murdered by a police officer in Minneapolis after being arrested in 2020. People were censured as racist for not supporting the BLM organization or philosophy. A closer inspection revealed a movement espousing Marxist ideals, the demise of the nuclear family, and pro-abortion and antisemitic views.

A battle against biblical beliefs is being waged on the issue of LGBTQ (lesbian, gay, bisexual, transgender, and queer or questioning). A growing number of U.S. states officially recognize three genders: male, female, and nonbinary/undesignated. Hot topics are debated, like the national recognition of same-sex marriage, the "drag queen story hours" held in public libraries for children ages three to eleven, and the acceptance of males who identify as females in women's sports. "Gender-affirming" hormone therapy and surgeries have increased in recent years, even for children.

Churches and places of worship are not exempt from the spirit of offense. Most pastors admit the inevitability of some congregants becoming offended. The sermon was too long; it needed to have more Bible verses; it needed to have fewer Bible verses; it confronted culture too directly. The music was too loud; the music was too hip; the music was too old-fashioned. The lights were too bright; the lights were too dim. The people were unfriendly. The pastor did not greet you, or, worse, did not remember your name.

Being offended ranks near the top of the reasons people leave a church, either to find a more suitable place to worship or to join the ranks of the "church of the unchurched."

More serious offenses are also rampant in the Church, to the point of splitting congregations and entire denominations. Many progressive Christians approve of abortion, living together outside of marriage, same-sex marriage, and the ordination of acting lesbians and homosexuals. Paul Chappell, president and founder of West Coast Baptist College, writes:

> There is a real need in our day for biblical Christians to be alert to worldly philosophies that masquerade as truth. I am

concerned for the future orthodoxy of Christians who seek influence and ideas from those who are swayed by woke ideas.[5]

How can we stand in the freedom of truth and not be offended by an increasingly hostile culture with ungodly ideas? That is the question we will explore in this chapter.

What *Is* Offense?

Offense is being bothered, annoyed, or resentful because of behavior perceived as done against you or actions not taken as expected. In the New Testament, the word *offense* comes from the Greek word *skandalon*, which was initially a movable stick with bait used to lure animals into a trap. Later the word came to mean a snare or stumbling block.[6] Offense can grow into anger, jealousy, strife, and bitterness. It hinders proper thought and conduct and blocks blessings.

Betrayal trauma can occur if someone you are close to has violated your trust or well-being. Jesus suffered betrayal by one of His disciples, Judas, and was actually betrayed by a kiss as Judas identified Him to the Roman soldiers in the Garden of Gethsemane. But Jesus, sinless in every way, did not give in to a sense of offense during this betrayal.

That cannot be said of many who suffer betrayal at the hands of family members, business associates, romantic partners, or friends. Offense can remain wedged in one's heart, supported by pride or self-justification. John Bevere, author of *The Bait of Satan*, a book about offense that has sold more than six million copies, states, "There is a false sense of self-protection in harboring an offense. It keeps you from seeing your own character flaws because the blame is deferred to another."[7]

Signs of Offense

There are many signs of being offended:

+ Closing your spirit and hardening your receptivity to a person or organization.
+ Leaving a church, seeking a divorce, quitting a job, or ceasing communication. (I recognize that these actions are sometimes required, but if so, it is important to remain free of offense and with as healthy a departure as possible.)
+ Being guarded and unwilling to share your heart freely.
+ Controlling people and situations to avoid contact.
+ Engaging in strained communication filled with defensive, argumentative, or sarcastic speech.
+ Resisting touch or hugs with family or in close friendships when that would be normal behavior.
+ Demonstrating pride, elevating yourself above the person or organization.
+ Isolating yourself to avoid more hurt, shame, and rejection.

Prophetic leader Kathy DeGraw says:

Offense is like an automatic weapon. Once you pull the trigger, it keeps firing. Unless properly identified and repentance and change come forth, the spirit of offense will continue to cause chaos and destroy relationships.[8]

This is why it is critical to identify and deal with offense in our lives—so we can live free from it and not allow it to entangle us as Jesus' return approaches.

The biblical patriarch Joseph (whom we looked at in chapter 3) had reason to hold residual offense toward his brothers, who had sold him into slavery. Yet he was able to say:

"Do not . . . be grieved or angry with yourselves because you sold me here; for God sent me before you to preserve life. . . . So now it was not you who sent me here, but God."

Genesis 45:5, 8

Because Joseph did not harbor bitterness or offense in his heart, he was able to rise from the pit to prison to the palace. Because he was free of offense, he could welcome his brothers and family to Egypt during the famine and care for them, allowing the children of Jacob to become the nation of Israel and prosper from seventy people to several million.

The young man David, future king of Israel, was sent by his father to take provisions to his brothers on the battle line with the Philistines. David arrived just in time to hear the giant Goliath taunting the Hebrew army. When David inquired about the giant, his oldest brother, Eliab, accused him of pride and insolence. Instead of being offended, David said, "What have I done now?" (1 Samuel 17:29). He went on to kill Goliath with a single stone, eventually becoming a great king and a forefather of the Messiah.

True champions will overcome the many opportunities that arise to be offended.

Biblical Examples

The Bible has numerous examples of the spirit of offense at work. Cain was offended and angry that his brother Abel's sacrifice, unlike his, was accepted by God, leading to the murder of his brother (see Genesis 4). Joseph's brothers were offended by his dreams of grandeur, his favor with their father, Jacob, and his coat of many colors, leading them to throw him into a pit and sell him into slavery (see Genesis 37). Aaron and Miriam were offended that Moses had married an Ethiopian woman, and they began to question Moses' leadership: "Has the LORD indeed spoken only through Moses? Has He not spoken through us also?" (Numbers 12:2). The Lord's anger was aroused against them, and Miriam was struck with leprosy for seven days. Job's wife was offended by God for all the troubles they were enduring, and encouraged her husband, "Curse God and die!" (Job 2:9).

A biblical example of offense spanning years is found in the family of David after he became king. David's oldest son, Amnon, loved Tamar, David's daughter by another wife, and devised a crafty plan to have the king instruct his half-sister to make and deliver food to Amnon while he was presumably sick in bed. Amnon used the occasion to rape Tamar, then shame her even more by coming to hate her and banning her from his presence. King David heard about it and was "very angry" (2 Samuel 13:21), but there is no record of him punishing Amnon.

Meanwhile Tamar lived, desolate, in the house of her brother Absalom, David's third son, who was deeply offended by Amnon's sin. Absalom did not speak to his brother for two years—until he murdered him and fled to Geshur. Even when David's army captain, Joab, got the king to bring Absalom back to Jerusalem after three years, David did not speak to him for two more years. Absalom finally prevailed on Joab to restore him to David's presence, and "then the king kissed Absalom" (2 Samuel 14:33).

But Absalom's offended spirit and devious ways later manifested in treason against his father, as he stole the hearts of the people and took over the kingdom for a time, until Joab killed Absalom in battle (see 2 Samuel 18).

An offended heart not dealt with speedily can brew and simmer, concocting evil plans of revenge.

Digging Deep into God's Love

In Matthew 24:10, after speaking of the signs of the end of the age, Jesus warned, "Many will be offended, will betray one another, and will hate one another." In verses 9–12 Jesus spoke of persecution, offense, betrayal, hatred, false prophets, deception, lawlessness, and that "the love of many will grow cold" (verse 12)—in that order.

Is it possible that these signs have a domino effect in which offense at persecution leads to betrayal, hatred, deception, lawlessness, and a cold heart?

Each Sabbath rest day, I read a portion of two books stationed on a coffee table in my living room: *Foxe: Voices of the Martyrs* and *Extreme Devotion*. Both books are published by Voice of the Martyrs, an organization started by Richard Wurmbrand, an evangelical Lutheran priest in Communist Romania and professor from a Jewish family who was imprisoned and tortured for his faith. The books tell the stories of believers, from ancient to modern day, who sacrificed everything for Christ. As I read each story, I am gripped by the fact that these ones who paid the ultimate price did so with hearts free of offense. Often, as they endured persecution, they forgave and prayed for their tormentors and executioners. They echo the words of Jesus as He hung on the cross: "Father, forgive them, for they do not know what they do" (Luke 23:34).

Sabina (Oster) Wurmbrand, Richard's Jewish wife, lost her mother, father, three younger sisters, and nine-year-old brother to brutal murder in a Nazi concentration camp during World War II. Yet she and Richard later welcomed into their home a Nazi officer who had worked at the very concentration camp where her family members had been exterminated. When the officer saw their forgiveness and love for him, he became a Christian. Sabina was to spend three years in prison and slave labor camps, where women were humiliated and beaten brutally. Yet she was known as a friend to all, who always had a kind word. Many lives were touched by her unconditional love.[9]

Corrie ten Boom has been a heroine to me since I was a child. I have read all her books and visited the Ten Boom Museum in Haarlem, the Netherlands, numerous times. The book *The Hiding Place*, as well as the movie with the same name, shares the story of Corrie and some family members imprisoned for hiding and saving the lives of Jews during the Nazi occupation of the Netherlands. Corrie and her sister Betsie were imprisoned in various camps, including the notorious women's concentration camp Ravensbrück, where Betsie perished.

Corrie's ability to dig deep into the love and forgiveness of God led her to help many women while imprisoned and go on to visit sixty nations over 33 years, spreading the message of forgiveness, hope, salvation, and living with an unoffended heart, even during the most horrific circumstances.

Righteous Offense

The thinking that one should not say anything that might be construed as offensive has pervaded our culture, including the Church. Yet the truth can stir offense. Jesus Himself was called "a stone of stumbling and a rock of offense" (1 Peter 2:8) because He spoke the truth and confronted religious and cultural lies. He stated, "Blessed is he who is not offended because of Me" (Matthew 11:6).

Renowned pastor and author A. W. Tozer stated, "Wherever I am, whatever I am doing, I hope and pray to God that I will have the courage to stand up for the real Jesus of the New Testament, regardless of whom I offend."[10] And the following statement is attributed to celebrated eighteenth-century preacher George Whitefield: "It is a poor sermon that gives no offense—that neither makes the hearer displeased with himself nor with the preacher."[11]

I heard a story about a class taught by a pastor in which an attendee piped up, "I was offended by something you said in last week's session." She was objecting to the statistics the pastor had shared that children growing up in two-parent homes have a better chance of living meaningful, godly lives. Because she was a single mother, she took issue with an observation that made her feel uncomfortable. It did not matter that facts had supported the pastor's statement.

This gets at today's reality of heightened sensitivities and the rise of political correctness, which we discussed at the beginning of this chapter. At times there is a fine line between being mindlessly offensive and tactfully truthful. But if there is a particular spirit behind offense, which I believe there is, it appears there has been an unleashing of the hordes of hell in this area. What the world sometime considers hate speech is only truth spoken that counters another person's beliefs and to which he or she objects, thus declaring it "hate speech."

We often quote Jesus' words, "You will know the truth, and the truth will set you free" (John 8:32 NIV). But the way we learn the truth is found in the context of Jesus' words: "If you hold to my teaching, you are really my disciples. *Then* you will know the truth, and the truth will set you free" (John 8:31–32 NIV, emphasis added). Freedom comes through the truth, which comes through obedience to Jesus; and hearing the truth can hurt and cause offense—if we let it.

Neuroscientist and philosopher Sam Harris said:

> I think the need is to be able to talk about the most important questions in human life without losing our connection to one another. . . . We need to be able to hear people out. We need to be able to reason about everything."[12]

Yes, we must be able to listen to each other and not cut people off if they say something we do not like. By the same token, if God is leading us to say something in love to another person, we must not hold back for fear of offending.

Jesus was not bothered when He offended those who were off course in life. When His disciples told him that the Pharisees were offended at His teaching, He replied, "Let them alone. They are blind leaders of the blind. And if the blind leads the blind, both will fall into a ditch" (Matthew 15:14).

At times offense is inevitable in the light of revealing truth. While we do not seek purposely to offend, and while we are to treat others the way we want to be treated, we must adhere to biblical truth.

Residual Offense

Once I heard a speaker use the term *residual offense*, which pierced my heart. The premise is that we can be offended and carry a low residual offense toward someone and not even realize it. Judgments we hold, lack of full forgiveness, harboring bitterness—all these are pillars supporting residual offense.

My husband and I were raised on different socioeconomic levels. John's family struggled financially, whereas my dad, who as I mentioned earlier was a successful farmer and real-estate broker, drove a new Cadillac and paid us kids reasonable wages for working on the farm. As a result, John's and my approaches to money differed greatly. It has taken years of prayer, healing, and communication to reach a healthy consensus on how to be financially responsible while still taking vacations and enjoying life.

Years ago the Lord revealed to me that I was holding residual offense against John for how he dealt with money. I was judging John as being stingy or lacking generosity; and with that set of lenses, I was unable to focus on the ways John was wise in financial prudence. Rather, I saw the ways he wanted to operate with what I viewed as control over what I could spend.

If we are offended by one another in marriage, it is a trap of darkness and of the evil one to divide us.

With the conviction of the Holy Spirit, I forgave John for where I felt he erred in finances. I repented for judging John in this area and for harboring residual offense. And I asked the Lord to purify my heart. It really made a difference. Although I am still more inclined than John is to plan a vacation or spend money with my daughters or friends at a coffee shop, we have experienced financial peace in our marriage and financial blessings as a result of walking in unity in this area.

Offense wants to creep into every relationship, and we must guard against it so we can live free of offense, in order to fulfill the purpose of God in our relationships.

Steps to Freedom

How do we identify and combat a spirit of offense? The apostle Paul explains in Philippians 1:9–11:

> This I pray, that your love may abound still more and more in knowledge and all discernment, that you may approve the things that are excellent, that you may be sincere and without offense till the day of Christ, being filled with the fruits of righteousness which are by Jesus Christ, to the glory and praise of God.

Those longing to have hearts free of dark influences, who want to fulfill their destiny and be useful to God, must overcome offense. It is imperative that we nip offense in the bud when it seeks to grow in our hearts. It is like a deadly cancer that, given opportunity, will grow and infect every area of our lives—emotions, relationships, health, and spirituality.

Jesus wants to free us so we can enjoy the fullness of life He has planned for us, and so we can fulfill His commission to reach the world before He returns. Offense only gets in the way of that.

So how can you be free of offense? I have three recommendations.

1. Let It Go

Let it go and trust in God's justice. A friend once said to me, "Offense never lets you go. You have to let *it* go." Deciding we will no longer get stuck in the trap of offense, we must purposely let it go. Extending forgiveness to the one who caused the offense is a crucial initial step to freedom, whether or not the offender ever apologizes.

Forgiveness sets one free of the ties that bind, and by letting go, the offended refuses to let herself be held captive by the offender's unwillingness to repent. It is hard to let go if we have no assurance of justice for the wrong that has been done. Rest assured that letting the offense go through forgiveness does not let the person off the hook; it just lets *you* off the hook to get justice for yourself for the offense. By forgiving the other person, you relieve yourself of that responsibility and turn it over to the Lord.

It is amazing what happens when you let God have His way instead of trying to work it out yourself. And when you extend mercy to those who do not deserve it, you will receive the mercy you do not deserve.

2. Receive God's Love

Grasping how much our Father in heaven loves us through abiding daily in His presence, meditating on His Word, and seeking our true identity as beloved sons and daughters before Him fills a deep void in our hearts that helps us overcome every obstacle in life.

One of the declarations I say to myself every day is this: "I am defined by my Father in heaven." Life will bring unfair treatment, but I can let it roll off instead of getting hooked. Proverbs 19:11 (NIV) says, "A person's wisdom yields patience; it is to one's glory to overlook an offense."

3. Pray for the Person

A third key to freeing ourselves of the hurt another has inflicted is to pray for that person. Here is what Jesus said:

> "I say to you, love your enemies, bless those who curse you, do good to those who hate you, and pray for those who spitefully use you and persecute you."
>
> Matthew 5:44

Suppose we begin to pray for the one who offended us, even if we do not think of that person as an enemy. When we do this, we release the blessing and freedom of the Lord over our lives and help change the other person's life to come under heavenly influence.

So do not hold an offense in your heart. Offense is a waste of emotional energy that yields no good fruit, and actually yields bad fruit, as we prepare to see Jesus and welcome His return. Jesus is expecting a Bride free of offense, free in her identity, and free to love Him with all her heart, mind, soul, and strength.

PRAYER

Father, set me free from the trap of offense. Fill my heart with the warmth of Your love. Let me be a true champion who rises above the many opportunities to be offended. I pray the words of the apostle Paul: "I myself always strive to have a conscience without offense toward God and men" (Acts 24:16).

7

FROM BITTERNESS
TO FORGIVENESS

Why should we hold onto the sins of others while our
own sins have been cast into the depths of the sea?

Corrie ten Boom, *Amazing Love*

Recently, while I was in prayer, a Scripture came to
me out of the blue. It was Psalm 103:12: "As far as
the east is from the west, so far has He removed our
transgressions from us." Over and over this resonated within
my heart. I was not aware of any sin I had committed recently.
Yet I felt this was a word the Lord wanted to highlight for
many. Then another phrase came, causing my tears to flow:
Forgiveness is beautiful.

Indeed, forgiveness *is* beautiful because it is the hinge for
the doorway of salvation, for us to spend this life and through

eternity in relationship with the Beautiful One. It is also glorious as the entrance to healing and reconciliation in all relationships scarred by sin.

Here are portions of King David's psalm of repentance:

> Wash me, and I shall be whiter than snow. Make me hear joy and gladness, that the bones You have broken may rejoice. . . . Create in me a clean heart, O God. . . . Restore to me the joy of Your salvation. . . . The sacrifices of God are a broken spirit, a broken and a contrite heart—these, O God, You will not despise.
>
> Psalm 51:7–8, 10, 12, 17

Getting free of the weight of sin and angst to receive joy and peace is worth more than gold.

The utmost importance of forgiveness was spoken by Jesus in Matthew 6:14–15:

> "If you forgive men their trespasses, your heavenly Father will also forgive you. But if you do not forgive men their trespasses, neither will your Father forgive your trespasses."

Forgiveness is not only beautiful but also not optional for the victorious Christian life.

In Matthew 18, after Jesus taught continuous forgiveness, even "up to seventy times seven" (verse 22), He told the parable of the unforgiving servant. The unjust servant who was forgiven a large debt—perhaps a million dollars in today's money—but who did not forgive a fellow servant who owed him a small sum opened himself to being delivered "to the torturers" (verse 34). Jesus' parable ends with this sober statement: "So My heavenly Father also will do to you if each of you, from his heart, does not forgive his brother his trespasses" (verse 35).

I believe "the torturers" are likely demons. Unforgiveness opens the door to oppression from the demonic realm and causes us to be "tied" to the person we hold in unforgiveness.

In the next chapter, "From Orphan Heart to Sonship," I recount my journey of forgiving my father and repenting of connected "bitter root judgments"—which was life-changing and set me on the road to marrying the godly husband I have and living free of bondage, so I would not repeat destructive family patterns. (We will talk about "a root of bitterness" in the next section.)

Demonstrating Forgiveness

Jesus demonstrated the most profound act of forgiveness when, dying on the cross, He uttered these words: "Father, forgive them, for they do not know what they do" (Luke 23:34).

Forgiveness is a decision of the will and not a feeling. We obey the directive of the Lord to forgive whether or not we feel like it and no matter the offense committed. Our emotions often catch up after we make the choice to forgive.

John Perkins

Born in 1930, John Perkins is an American minister, author, community developer, and African-American civil rights activist. A third-grade dropout, he has received seventeen honorary doctorate degrees and has served on a Presidential Task Force for five U.S. presidents.

When he was just seven months old, living in Mississippi, his mother died of pellagra due to starvation. In 1947 his brother, a veteran of World War II, was killed by a police officer. John himself, following the arrest of students seeking the desegregation of an all-white Mississippi high school, was arrested and tortured by white police officers while in jail. But through his strong Christian faith, he rose above hatred to forgive the racist wrongs committed against him.

Even at this writing, John Perkins, now in his nineties, has worked tirelessly to reconcile the races and give practical help to the impoverished. In his 2018 book *One Blood*, a book he calls his final manifesto, Perkins states, "Forgiveness is the linchpin of reconciliation."[1]

Corrie ten Boom

I mentioned in the last chapter that Corrie ten Boom has been a hero of mine since I was a child. Two years after her time at the concentration camp, while speaking in a German church on the power of the love and forgiveness of God, Corrie saw a man in the audience who was one of the cruel prison guards at Ravensbrück. Afterward, she wanted to slip away from the meeting quietly, but this man came forward, extending his hand and asking, "Would you forgive me?"

Corrie describes what happens next:

"Jesus, help me!" I prayed silently. "I can lift my hand. I can do that much. You supply the feeling."

And so woodenly, mechanically, I thrust my hand into the one stretched out to me. And as I did, an incredible thing took place. The current started in my shoulder, raced down my arm, sprang into our joined hands. And then this healing warmth seemed to flood my whole being, bringing tears to my eyes.

"I forgive you, brother!" I cried. "With all my heart!"

For a long moment, we grasped each other's hands, the former guard and the former prisoner. I had never known God's love so intensely as I did then.[2]

Corrie ten Boom, a self-proclaimed "tramp for the Lord" who traversed the nations, sharing the way of salvation and the power of forgiveness, once stayed in the home of a Kansas farm family whose youngest daughter was about to graduate from high school. All planned to attend the graduation celebration—all except the older son, whom the father, in a fit of anger, had shown the door and forbidden ever to return.

The son lived on a nearby farm, and the farmer's wife was distraught about the fractured relationship.

Corrie had the opportunity to talk with the farmer as they rode horseback through the fields together. She talked with him about God's forgiveness and reminded him of the Lord's Prayer—that we must forgive if we have been forgiven.

Throughout the conversation, Corrie wrote later, she prayed against the "root of bitterness" that the biblical writer warned about—"[Look] carefully lest anyone fall short of the grace of God; lest any root of bitterness springing up cause trouble, and by this many become defiled" (Hebrews 12:15)—and she prayed that such a root would not win the conflict inside the farmer's heart.

They rode in silence for a while.

[Then] he said suddenly, "I'm going to see my son tonight. Will you go with me?"

And so we did. The older man was a bit uncomfortable as he stepped into the house. The son looked up in surprise. Then the father put his hand on the shoulder of the young man and said, "My boy, will you forgive me?"

I turned and walked quickly to the other side of the house, but I could still hear the son's reply, "But Father, I should ask you for forgiveness."

The graduation party was a great success.[3]

Binding and Loosing

A young man whom John and I knew while we pastored in Canada recounted that his father had been a difficult man who changed over time. This young man had attended the Catch the Fire School of Ministry in Toronto and learned about the Father heart of God and the way of forgiveness. When he worked through forgiving his father, he saw a softening in his dad's heart.

Later one of his sisters also went through the Catch the Fire School of Ministry and similarly worked through forgiveness, and they both noted that their dad changed for the better even more.

Later, a third sibling did the same. By this time, they said, their father was revolutionized.

How is that possible when the father never apologized for his wrongs? I believe his transformation took place because of the principle Jesus outlined in Matthew 16. Jesus and His disciples were at Caesarea Philippi, at the place known as the gates of Hades, where Greek gods were worshiped. Jesus asked His disciples who the people said He was. Peter answered that Jesus was "the Christ, the Son of the living God" (verse 16). Jesus commended him for this response, and went on:

> "On this rock [of revelation] I will build My church, and the gates of Hades shall not prevail against it. And I will give you the keys of the kingdom of heaven, and whatever you bind on earth will be bound in heaven, and whatever you loose on earth will be loosed in heaven."
>
> Matthew 16:18–19

Is it possible that when we release forgiveness over someone, "loosing" that person, he or she is in a position to become unbound from the wrong and more open to the working of the Holy Spirit? I believe so. And the person who gets particularly unbound is the person doing the forgiving! When we forgive from the heart, it is as if a weight has been lifted, or as if a repetitive soundtrack of negativity in the mind has been broken. Once "stuck," whether in our inability to get past emotional pain or to get on with our destiny, we can become unstuck when we offer forgiveness.

Forms of Forgiveness

Forgiveness takes different forms. We must forgive others for wrongs done against us. Sometimes we need to release God from our expectations of what He should have done or not done. (We will talk more on this in chapter 9.) And we may need to forgive ourselves for wrongs we have committed, which have cost us in some form.

Forgiving Ourselves

I realized in my early twenties that I had wasted some years in complacency in my relationship with the Lord. I had crossed over into the land of sin and self-will instead of God's will for my life. I asked the Lord to forgive me for three and a half wasted years in a wrong dating relationship. I had deep regret and repented. In love and kindness, the Lord forgave me and prompted me to forgive myself, get up, push *delete*, and go on in pursuit of Him.

That is precisely what I did, and I am grateful to this day for the Lord's admonition.

Not forgiving ourselves prompts us to distance ourselves from communion with the Father, as though we have to pay some penance for ill behavior. No, that is what Jesus did on the cross—He paid the price for sin so we can return to Him in fellowship.

Why remain in the distant court of isolation when we can move beyond the veil in nearness to the God of love?

Forgiving Adversaries

A test for every believer comes in the form of how we react to those who criticize us, slander us, or try to block us in some way. In other words, how do we respond to enemies or adversaries?

Jesus answered this question in Luke 6:27–31:

> "Love your enemies, do good to those who hate you, bless those who curse you, and pray for those who spitefully use you. To him who strikes you on the one cheek, offer the other also. And from him who takes away your cloak, do not withhold your tunic either. Give to everyone who asks of you. And from him who takes away your goods, do not ask them back. And just as you want men to do to you, you also do to them likewise."

If you are a follower of Jesus, forgiveness is not optional. But forgiveness is not the same as trust. At times trust needs to be rebuilt over time, such as when an offender is legitimately penitent and the relationship needs to be restored, such as in a marriage. At other times we need to protect ourselves, or others in our sphere of influence, from being hurt repeatedly by individuals needing character change.

When the hurt of wrong still lingers, praying for the perpetrator and speaking blessings over him or her is a key to freedom. In my journal I have written the names of those who have hurt me deeply. I pray for them every day (and hope they never read my journal!). These prayers have removed the sting of the betrayal or offense. Instead, legitimate love has budded, and in every case the relationship has been restored.

We may not feel as if others deserve to be forgiven for wrongs they have committed. We may even think that we ourselves are beyond grace. Yet the love of God filling us through His Spirit gives us an unearthly ability to let go, rip up the "I owe you," forgive others or ourselves, and let God turn it all around.

Jesus was anointed by the Father to pay the price of death so we can be forgiven and filled with the Spirit, to forgive others and ourselves. Jesus was sent

> "to heal the brokenhearted, to proclaim liberty to the captives, and the opening of the prison to those who are bound; to proclaim the acceptable year of the LORD, and the day of vengeance of our God; to comfort all who mourn, to console those who mourn in Zion, to give them beauty for ashes, the oil of joy for mourning, the garment of praise for the spirit of heaviness; that they may be called trees of righteousness, the planting of the LORD, that He may be glorified."
>
> . . . Instead of your shame you shall have double honor, and instead of confusion they shall rejoice in their portion. Therefore in their land they shall possess double; everlasting joy shall be theirs.
>
> Isaiah 61:1–3, 7

Indeed, forgiveness is a beautiful thing.

PRAYER

Lord, reveal any unforgiveness that I may be harboring in my life. I choose to forgive and trust You to help remove the hurt and injustice done. I also choose to forgive myself when I have sinned. Thank You for cleansing me through the power of forgiveness.

8

From Orphan Heart to Sonship

Behold what manner of love the Father has bestowed on us, that we should be called children of God!

1 John 3:1

God demonstrates His love of family through the Trinity. The Father has a Son, and both are in complete unity with the Holy Spirit. Each Person of the Trinity is coequal and coeternal, and they are family. As we seek to live life to the fullest and prepare for Jesus' return and our eternity, it behooves us to grasp what it means to be children of God.

We, too, are adopted as sons and daughters "according to the good pleasure of His will, to the praise of the glory of His grace, by which He made us accepted in the Beloved"

(Ephesians 1:5–6). Knowing the Father's love for us is foundational to a vibrant life in God. All of us are searching for significance. It is where we choose to find it that determines our outcome. Fathers give identity, and usually give their children their surname. Fathers help provide the lens through which, for better or worse, we see and relate to God as Father.

I have heard it said that, for each of us on earth, our father was the first man we knew, who set the tone for all the men who would come into our lives. Our dads were major forces in determining our self-esteem. The father-child relationship expands to thoughts, feelings, interactions, and behaviors. And though these often continue into adulthood and parenthood, many of us as adults no longer recognize our feelings and behaviors as connected to our fathers. But the truth is, whether we recognize it or not, our fathers have a strong voice in how we view ourselves in everything from relationships to job performance.

The effects of fatherlessness in society cause untold damage. Statistics show that, in the U.S., those raised in a fatherless home (more than eighteen million children) are four times more likely to live in poverty. Fatherless children are twice as likely to suffer from mental health problems. They make up 63 percent of youth suicides and 85 percent of the children who exhibit behavior disorders. Children from single-parent homes account for 70 percent of juveniles in state-operated institutions. According to one study, girls whose fathers left the home before they were five are eight times more likely to become pregnant as teenagers.[1]

Various studies have shown these statistics: 72 percent of adolescent murderers come from fatherless homes, and

80 percent of rapists with anger problems grew up without dads. Ninety percent of all homeless and runaway children are from fatherless homes, and 71 percent of high school dropouts.[2]

In his *New York Times* bestseller *The Body Keeps the Score*, Dr. Bessel van der Kolk outlines the deep wounding on the mind, emotions, development, and physical bodies of neglected and abused children. They carry a form of post-traumatic stress disorder, not unlike veterans of intense conflict in war. The cost to society in terms of treatment centers, medical care, and foster homes pales in comparison to the cost of quality of life for these scarred ones. In most cases, abusive or neglectful parents simply propagate what was done to them.[3]

Types of Fathers

Different father types influence sons and daughters in specific ways. Following is a summary of different expressions of fathering and their effects on offspring. It is important to note that these feelings carry into adulthood unless healing transpires.

Absent Father

A father's absence due to death, divorce, long work hours, a busy travel schedule, or leaving the family can result in feelings of neglect, rejection, and abandonment. Sons or daughters raised by an absent father may feel that God is distant and uninvolved. They may also strive for approval and feel they must make their own way in the world, as God will not come through for them. They often fear getting close to God due to the risk of abandonment.

Passive Father

The passive father is not responsive, involved, or active in his child's life. It is difficult to get his attention as he may be hidden behind a newspaper, television, or electronic device. The passive father rarely initiates affection, activities to do together, or pursuing his child's heart. He may be unemotional and withdrawn, finding it hard to express himself.

As a result of passive parenting, children can experience hidden anger or difficulty resolving problems or getting in touch with emotions. They may have trouble experiencing intimacy in relationships, including with God. They may feel they are on their own and that God will not protect them. They may face despondency, depression, and feeling "not good enough," striving to gain the father's and God's attention.

Performance-Oriented Father

This father has high standards, not tempered with enough love, nurture, or affection. He points to faults and failures in order to motivate success, and he rarely affirms strengths. He expresses love and affirmation only when the child has performed well according to his standards. A typical example is ignoring the A's on a report card but pointing out the one B, wondering why it is not an A.

The children of performance-oriented fathers can fear failure right into adulthood—not being "good enough." They may struggle with feeling they can never live up to God's standards, driven constantly to earn love and acceptance. They need to work harder, wear a mask, appear super-spiritual, and have little sense of rest. It is said that most people who suffer from depression have at least one performance-oriented parent.

Authoritarian Father

This father is a strict legalist who lives by the rules and has little ability to give intimacy and express love. He values obedience above relationship, truth above love. Approval comes by obeying the rules. This translates to offspring feeling that love and obedience are intertwined, and it can lead to fear, loss of motivation in life, and a lack of identity. His children can see God as the big cop in the sky, watching to make sure they obey the rules—and making it hard to develop a relationship with Him.

Abusive Father

The abusive father is angry and inflicts physical, emotional, verbal, or sexual abuse. This creates inner pain, fear, and insecurity. His children ask, "Is he in a good mood? Is he angry?" They are always aware of the emotional atmosphere when Dad is around. They need to keep the peace, and often feel they are walking on eggshells, since peace can be disrupted at the slightest mishap. They may feel it is their fault and find it hard to relax. They may feel guilt, shame, and a sense of worthlessness. It is common for them to try to shut down fear or turn to counterfeit affections to dull the pain. They may jump into a relationship with the first person who shows any form of "love," or they may turn to drugs, alcohol, or food. In terms of God, they may feel unsure of a relationship with Him or fear that He is angry. It is hard for them to relate to spiritual authority in the Church.

Good Father

This type of father pours out unconditional affirmation, love, and encouragement in concrete ways, even amid healthy discipline. He initiates a relationship with his child and communicates pride in him or her. He gives affirmation in hugs, kisses, touch, gifts, reassurance, and encouragement. He helps impart value, identity, and purpose. He comes to the rescue when needed. A good father talks openly about how much he loves his child, and he loves unconditionally, not based on performance, just as the Father said of Jesus: "This is my Son, whom I love; with him I am well pleased" (Matthew 3:17 NIV).

The offspring of such a parent will have greater confidence and ability to rebound after disappointment or rejection. He or she will connect more easily with the love of God.

My Story

The formative years of my life were a paradox. Fun times included living on a farm with ponies, horses, ducks, sheep, chickens, dogs, and cows as friends, and with the Canadian open fields as my playground. Farmwork needed constant attention, but the pool was waiting for a cool dive in the summer months. Winter brought massive snow mounds calling for us to toboggan or build a fort.

Family dynamics, however, were not so idyllic. Tension, fear, and angst were fueled by our often-angry father, who directed his explosive outbursts at my mother, me, or one of my six siblings. I, and at least some of my siblings, disliked my father and despised how he treated our mother. His moods oscillated, and he often took turns ostracizing one child. We often sought to keep our distance from him, walking on eggshells trying to prevent trouble.

When Sunday rolled around, we looked like the most together family, dressing well and going to the established

Dutch Canadian church. I thought life was normal in my family, which is often the case when you do not know anything different.

When I was around fifteen, I discovered that my father, raised in a family of sixteen children in the Netherlands, was the child particularly abused by his own father. Additionally (as I said in chapter 3), he lived under Nazi occupation in World War II during his formative years, witnessing many atrocities. Not having experienced healing from the pain of his past, my dad was living out what was done to him and his siblings.

At the same time, I started to realize there was something defective in my own character. Unforgiveness, bitterness, and dislike for my father contributed to my insecurity and lack of joy. I was living with an orphan heart.

Orphan or Adopted Child?

Before I return to my story, let's explore what an orphan heart is, so we can appreciate that we are not orphans but adopted children in the family of God. An orphan heart is often formed through neglect or abuse. He does not feel accepted or valued just as he is. She does not feel that she belongs. This can lead to insecurity, low self-confidence, and the need to strive for approval.

One does not need to be parentless to display orphan-like tendencies. An orphan heart can manifest itself when there has been a disconnect from one or both parents or when there have been adverse experiences in the foundational years.

Contrasting Hearts

Having now graduated to heaven, Jack Frost, Bible teacher and founder of Shiloh Place Ministries, contrasted the orphan heart with the spirit of sonship (a term equally valid for both sons and daughters). Here is some of what he concluded.[4]

Orphan Heart	Heart of Sonship
Sees God as slave driver	Sees God as loving Father
Independent, self-reliant	Interdependent, acknowledging need
Lives by the love of law	Lives by the law of love
Insecure; lacks peace	Secure; experiences rest and peace
Strives for the praise and approval of others	Feels accepted in God's love and justified by grace
Motivated to serve from a need for personal achievement, seeking to impress God and others—or else not motivated to serve at all	Motivated to serve from gratitude for being unconditionally loved and accepted by God
Performs Christian disciplines out of duty, to earn God's favor	Performs Christian disciplines out of pleasure and delight
"Must" be holy and pure to win God's favor, thus increasing personal shame and guilt	"Wants" to be holy and pure to nurture an intimate relationship with God
Rejects self after comparison with others	Feels positive, affirmed, valued by God
Seeks comfort in counterfeit affections, addictions, compulsions, or else in escapism, busyness, and hyper-religious activity	Seeks times of quietness and solitude to rest in the Father's presence and love

Orphan Heart	Heart of Sonship
Competitive in peer relationships; jealous over others' success and position	Humble in peer relationships, valuing others and rejoicing in their success and blessings
Exposing others' faults, trying to look good by making them look bad	Covering over others' faults, seeking to restore them in love and gentleness
Distrusts authorities, seeing them as sources of pain, and lacking a heart attitude of submission	Respects authorities, honoring and seeing them as ministers of good
Must be right; feelings are easily hurt; spirit closed to admonition and discipline	Receives advice as a blessing to expose and put to death faults and weaknesses
Guarded and conditional in expressing love	Open, patient, affectionate, and giving
Sees God's presence as conditional and distant	Sees God's presence as close and intimate
Experiences bondage	Experiences liberty
Feels like a servant or enslaved person	Feel like a son or daughter
Spiritually ambitious; hungry for spiritual achievement and willing to strive for it; wants to be seen and counted among the mature	Wants to experience the Father's unconditional love and acceptance daily, and then represent His love to others
Views the future as a fight for what one can get	Views the future as an inheritance released by sonship

Adoption

I have often heard John say to our children over the years, "You have two fathers, one on earth and one in heaven." It may be, at these times, that one of our children was asking

123

for a purchase beyond our budget or an insight beyond our understanding, and John was reminding the children of their heavenly Father's infinite resources or limitless wisdom. It would have led to a time of prayer to invoke the supernatural intervention of a divine Father who was very near.

For many, the concept of an involved, benevolent, loving Father in heaven seems as far away as the moon. Yet the heavenly Father longs to heal all the brokenhearted, draw us close, and hold us in His embrace.

Ephesians 1:5 says that God "predestined us to adoption as sons by Jesus Christ to Himself, according to the good pleasure of His will." We have another bloodline, a different family into which we are welcomed. This new bloodline was made possible through the shed blood of Jesus on the cross. His sacrifice paid the price to take us from being sinful, rejected orphans and outcasts to being sons and daughters in a royal family. The Father asks in Isaiah 49:15–16:

"Can a woman forget her nursing child, and not have compassion on the son of her womb? Surely they may forget, yet I will not forget you. See, I have inscribed you on the palms of My hands."

Similarly, Jesus said, reflecting the love of the Father, "I will not leave you orphans; I will come to you" (John 14:18).

The Road to Healing

Once a person is grafted into a new family, moving from living like an orphan to living like a son or daughter does not happen in a moment. There is a process in this journey of the heart. Unlike deliverance from demonic spirits, one does not "cast out" an orphan heart. Instead, it needs to be "loved out." It also requires choices.

Forgiveness

The first choice we make on the road to healing is to forgive our fathers and other authority figures for the ways they did not represent God as Father. Forgiveness, as I mentioned in the previous chapter, is an essential key to healing and freedom. It cuts the chains that tie us to the person or offense. It sets us free and removes the enemy's legal rights to have access to us. This includes forgiving sins of *commission* (acts done against us), such as emotional, physical, and sexual abuse; and forgiving sins of *omission* (acts not done that should have been), such as lack of affirmation, hugs, and healthy play together.

My process of forgiving my father began at age fourteen from a strong sense the Lord gave me that I needed to forgive. I often wonder how many times I have forgiven my father. I identify with Peter asking Jesus how often he must forgive. Jesus responded, "I do not say to you, up to seven times, but up to seventy times seven" (Matthew 18:22). In other words, you forgive and never stop forgiving, whether you feel like it or not. It starts with a choice. Often, at a later date, feelings will catch up as you realize just how freeing it is to forgive someone.

I discovered two aspects of forgiveness. First, you do not need someone to ask you for forgiveness before you forgive. Jesus was on the cross asking the Father to forgive those crucifying Him. They certainly did not ask for forgiveness. Second, general forgiveness is okay, but forgiveness for specific sins can help free you from the effects or patterns of those sins.

As my six children were growing up, one of them would often spill a drink at the lunch or dinner table. I found myself flustered by this and cleaning up the spill impatiently while admonishing the guilty child to "be more careful." After I questioned the Lord about why I was so bothered by frequent spills, I sensed the gentle voice of my heavenly Father reminding me that when I was a child and spilled at the table, my dad would become angry and upset. I was reacting the same way some thirty years later. When I specifically forgave my dad for his anger in those situations and asked the Lord to forgive me for judging my dad and then doing the same thing, something lifted off my life. I no longer got upset when one of our children spilled. A cyclic pattern was broken.

Breaking Bitter Root Judgments

Breaking bitter root judgments and expectancies is the second step on the road to healing. These are often the driving force behind recurring negative patterns. Hebrews 12:15 (NASB) says, "See to it that no one comes short of the grace of God; that no root of bitterness springing up causes trouble, and by it many be defiled."

Bitter roots come from our sinful response to hurts, such as bitterness, resentment, and negative attitudes. They also come when we make condemning judgments of people and refuse or find ourselves unable to forgive. Bitter roots are not what is done against us; they are our sinful reactions.

Just as there are laws in nature, such as the law of gravity, there are spiritual laws at work, even if we are unaware of them. If you jump off a roof, the law of gravity will cause you to fall to the ground. Similarly, if you defy spiritual laws without intervention, you will suffer consequences. Here are three of those laws.

JUDGMENT

The Law of Judgment mandates that in areas where you have judged someone, you will be judged and will very often do the same things. Matthew 7:1–2 (NIV) says, "Do not judge, or you too will be judged. For in the same way you judge others, you will be judged, and with the measure you use, it will be measured to you." Romans 2:1 reveals that we are on track to do the same things we judge someone else for: "You are inexcusable, O man, whoever you are who judge, for in whatever you judge another you condemn yourself; for you who judge practice the same things."

SOWING AND REAPING

The Law of Sowing and Reaping means that you will reap or be given in turn what you sow or give. "Do not be deceived; God cannot be mocked. A man reaps what he sows" (Galatians 6:7 NIV). Additionally, just as one planted kernel of corn produces a much greater yield, what we sow will grow, as Hosea 8:7 indicates: "They sow the wind, and reap the whirlwind."

HONOR

The Law of Honor means you will be blessed in ways you have shown honor.

I discussed in chapter 3 that when our family moved back to my hometown in Canada, where my parents still lived, I rediscovered the fifth of the Ten Commandments:

> "Honor your father and your mother, as the LORD your God has commanded you, that your days may be long, and that it may be well with you in the land which the LORD your God is giving you."
>
> Deuteronomy 5:16

As we realize that these laws work together, we see bitter root judgments acting like boomerangs, returning to us. If we judge our mothers for being negative, for example, we can inadvertently become negative ourselves, even though that is not our desire. A bitter root in our hearts is at work, fueled by judgment. It will gain momentum when sowed and will produce dishonor, which does not bode well for our lives.

THE ROOT AND THE FRUIT

When we judge someone, we expect something from that person and view him or her through a set of lenses, and that is all we can see. A bitter root expectancy is a habitual way of viewing how things will go for us. It acts like a self-fulfilling prophecy.

I had judged my father as being mean and unkind. That was rooted in unforgiveness and bitterness in my heart, such that it expanded to a judgment that went like this: "All men are mean and unkind." The kinds of guys I attracted as a young woman were mean and unkind, even though they may have seemed the opposite initially. My judgment could have fueled this behavior in some of these men.

Of my dad's twelve sisters raised by my abusive grandfather, eleven married disagreeable men. As a teenager, I was on track with this family curse in the men I dated. My dad was a tall Dutchman. I avoided all potential suitors of Dutch heritage. Yet I gravitated toward men who were similar in character. The "nice" guys never attracted me. It was as if an invisible sign on my head said, *All you dysfunctional men, I'm attracted to you.*

The family curse was being propagated. I was stuck, broken, and searching for love in all the wrong places. Why do children of alcoholics marry alcoholics? Why do those who were abused become abusers? These laws and principles are powerful, and I knew them too well. If you have the fruit, you have the root, and I had the fruit and root, and was not sure how to get free.

The Next Step

After a dream from the Lord revealing that the boyfriend I had been dating for three and half years was not for me, I finally ended that relationship. With a broken heart and an impassioned cry to the Lord, I asked for help to know whom He wanted me to marry.

In response, I heard His still, small voice say, *John.* Intrigued, I pressed further: "John who?" To which I heard the reply, *John Bootsma.*

I had not met a John Bootsma and dismissed this as my imagination. My oldest sister had married a guy named John, so there were enough Johns in the family. Furthermore, Bootsma is a Dutch name!

Yet within months, a good-looking guy my age named John Bootsma moved to my city and started attending my church. *Hmmm. God, was that You?*

Sure enough, John expressed interest in me, even telling me soon after that he knew he was to marry a woman named Patricia.

Great! We know God wants us to be married—but we should get to know each other. The problem was, John was one of those nice guys who opened the car door, closed the car door, gave flowers, and was sensitive and kind—the very kind of guy I was never attracted to.

After a time of not seeing John, the Lord orchestrated the return of my spiritual mother and pastor, Carol Arnott, who had been traveling. She was loaded with recordings of teachings on inner healing, which I gladly devoured. I recognized the principles I had violated in unforgiveness, judgments, and vows.

Breaking Inner Vows

Inner vows are the determinations, statements, or directives our minds and hearts make in response to being hurt. They are like the train tracks on which our life runs, holding us to feel, think, and act in specific ways.

Matthew 5:37 says, "Let your 'Yes' be 'Yes,' and your 'No,' 'No.' For whatever is more than these is from the evil one." Even "good" vows can be harmful, as they push us to do the right thing for the wrong reasons, and to do them in our strength instead of through the power of God.

Examples of inner vows include "I will not let a woman near my heart again." "I will never again allow myself to be embarrassed." "I will never have children." "I will always be free of addictions, unlike my dad." "I will always do well on tests at school."

Prayer is needed to invite the Holy Spirit into the garden of our hearts to reveal vows we have made. Then we must confess and repent of them and break our agreement with those vows.

One of my inner vows was "I'll never marry anyone like my dad." Another one was "I will never marry a Dutchman." Those vows were rooted in ungodly judgments and needed to be broken.

After I did so, Carol prayed with me to take authority over those vows to break their effects on my life.

I felt the change! I was no longer bound by the vows that had tied me to dark patterns. It was time to repent.

Repentance

I confessed and repented for my sinful reactions to childhood trauma, family patterns, and judgments. I forgave my father from my heart. The power of judgments and bitter roots holding them in place was broken as Carol prayed for me.

Prayers to demolish spiritual structures holding judgments and reaping the same preceded blessings of resurrection to reverse the old patterns and receive new ways of relating to others—specifically, for me, with men.

Deliverance

Demonic strongholds can be given legal access to us through willful sin, family curses, and unforgiveness (see Matthew 18:34–35).

Once I had done the hard work of facing my sinful reactions to past experiences, confessing them, and repenting, it was an easier job to cast out demonic structures and oppressive spirits that had been given access to my life.

Obtaining freedom from oppression was a game-changer in my life. I looked at my future husband and fell into a deep, healthy love that has only grown today after more than 34 years of marriage.

Choosing Sonship

A visiting speaker to our church years ago asked a question during a talk on the Father heart of God. "At what point," he asked the congregation, "did you cease to be a son or a daughter?"

I did not understand why, but that question bothered me. I went home, got alone with God, and began to pray. That is when the Lord revealed something to me I had forgotten.

When I was fourteen, I saw my dad's parenting as so inconsistent and troubling that I chose not to need a dad, and I became very independent. Getting a job, I bought my own toiletries and clothes. Like my siblings, I called my dad by his first name, Bernie. Later I paid my way through university and bought my own car. When John and I married, we paid for our wedding. Even when my dad tried to father me in his way, I resisted, full of an orphan heart.

Now, although I was a wife and mother, the Lord revealed to me that the decision I had made long ago was still affecting my life on three levels. It was affecting my relationship with Father God. I knew He loved me, but it felt like a distant relationship. Second, I was keeping my spiritual father at arm's length. And third, my decision from long ago was influencing my relationship with my dad, whom I had forgiven but whom I did not particularly like or want to spend time with.

I knew what was required of me: repentance. So I repented to the Lord for being distant, not unlike the Prodigal Son in Luke 15. Then I repented to my spiritual father. He was on a long trip, so I wrote him a heartfelt email, to which he responded kindly. And the hardest thing I did was go to my dad and ask him to forgive me for not being a good daughter. Dad did not understand this turn in me, but he forgave me.

Repenting for not acting like a son or daughter, and choosing sonship, launched for me a whole new level of walking in the revelation of sonship and knowing who I was as a beloved daughter to God, to my spiritual father, and to my dad.

Romans 8:14–15 (NIV) says:

Those who are led by the Spirit of God are the children of God. The Spirit you received does not make you slaves, so that you live in fear again; rather, the Spirit you received brought about your adoption to sonship.

Communion with the Father

I have heard it said, "We will walk with the Father as much as we talk to the Father."

A deep connection with our Father in heaven involves communication, which comes when we position ourselves in prayer, devour His Word, and listen for His voice. Jesus said, "As the Father loved Me, I also have loved you; abide in My love" (John 15:9). That is incredible if we grasp this. As much as the Father loves the Son, He loves us. It takes a lifetime of meditating on this truth to unpack it.

One of my daily declarations to Jesus is: "You feel about me as the Father feels about You. I am Your beloved. You delight in me. I am accepted. I belong. I am significant. I am defined by my Father in heaven."

Whether we are eight years old or 88, we need a Father. And we have a Father who loves us more than life itself.

So choose to be a son or a daughter of the One who longs to draw you not only into your future home in heaven but into the home of His heart right now.

——————— PRAYER ———————

Lord, forgive me for any way I have lived with an orphan heart. I choose sonship. I thank You for being my Father. I receive Your unconditional love.

9

FROM TRIALS TO TRIUMPH

I will lift up my eyes to the hills—from whence comes my help? My help comes from the LORD, who made heaven and earth.

Psalm 121:1–2

We have looked at some of the letters to the seven churches in Revelation 2 and 3—messages given by Jesus after He ascended to heaven and before He returns to earth to get His Bride. They were written not only to seven congregations in the Roman Empire, but also to individuals who are part of the global Church today. In each of these seven letters, a promise is attached for the one "who overcomes." In these promises, we see the ultimate reward for being an overcomer—being with Jesus for eternity.

These end-time messages were given because the Lord knew that believers then and now had hardships, trials, tests, and pain to overcome. It is not a matter of whether we will experience difficulties, but how we respond to them.

Hurts in life have the potential to make us better or bitter. We can choose to run to a loving Father and be embraced in His love, or we can run the other way. Sadly some have walked away from their faith due to significant hurts in life.

A significant blow to my extended family came when my beloved niece passed suddenly into eternity at age forty. She had conquered breast cancer six years prior, yet she was gone after a roller-coaster ten-day battle with a rare blood disorder and cancerous lesions on her spine.

Blonde, beautiful, kind, and full of life, Shauna was one month shy of her planned wedding, leaving behind an eight-year-old daughter from a previous marriage. She had decorated and furnished the large home backing onto a golf course that she and her fiancé had purchased, ready for her and her daughter to move in after the wedding. Her close-knit family and her fiancé and daughter were left devastated. I had the privilege and weighty responsibility to conduct her funeral.

Tragically, eight months later, our family was struck with another disaster. My 48-year-old nephew, Jason, a sergeant in the Royal Canadian Mounted Police, on assignment in Quebec City to guard the Pope in his upcoming visit to the city in just a few days, collapsed and died while at the gym. No amount of resuscitation could bring him back. He left behind a wife and four children. The autopsy revealed no known cause of death—commonly referred to as sudden adult death syndrome.

Questions remain for us to grapple with under such circumstances. Why? Where was God? How can people so kind and good experience something so tragic? Since the introduction of sin to the Garden of Eden, we live in a fallen world subject to forces of evil and darkness.

But one thing becomes clear: We will not know all the answers to our questions this side of heaven. Isaiah 55:8–9 says:

> "My thoughts are not your thoughts, nor are your ways My ways," says the Lord. "For as the heavens are higher than the earth, so are My ways higher than your ways, and My thoughts than your thoughts."

Infirmities

Kathryn Kuhlman was an extraordinary prayer minister who, between the 1940s and 1970s, saw many miracles in her services. Multiple sclerosis spontaneously cured, the disappearance of rampant cancer, the healing of a lifelong crippling deformity, the desire to die being transformed into the will to live—these are just a few of the miracles manifested in this woman's meetings.

Yet Kathryn agonized over the many who attended her services and were not healed. In her book *God Can Do It Again*, she wrote:

> Why are not all healed? The only honest answer I can give is I do not know. And I am afraid of those who claim they do know. For only God knows, and who can fathom the mind of God? Who can understand His reasoning? . . .
>
> God does not have to prove Himself to anyone. . . . There are some things in life that will always be unanswerable because we see through a glass darkly. . . .
>
> If a man like Paul, after all his glorious revelations, did not have the answers for his own thorn in the flesh, then how

can we expect to know the answers? God's answer to Paul is adequate to me, "My grace is sufficient for thee: for my strength is made perfect in weakness." Paul's answer to the world should become the password of every believer: "Most gladly, therefore, will I rather glory in my infirmities, that the power of Christ may rest upon me."[1]

Suffering

In everyday life as well as in challenging circumstances, we must turn to the authority of the Bible and find the truth therein.

The book of Job gives us a unique view of suffering. God called Job "a blameless and upright man, one who fears God and shuns evil" (Job 1:8). Satan came before God, saying, in effect, "The only reason Job walks with You is because You have blessed him and put a hedge of protection around him. Remove that protection, and he will curse You."

When the Lord allowed that hedge to be partially removed, Satan caused Job's property and livestock to be destroyed—and, more importantly, his ten children to be killed when a wind collapsed the house they were in. Yet this was Job's reaction:

> Then Job arose, tore his robe, and shaved his head; and he fell to the ground and worshiped. And he said, "Naked I came from my mother's womb, and naked shall I return there. The Lord gave, and the Lord has taken away; blessed be the name of the Lord." In all this Job did not sin nor charge God with wrong.
>
> Job 1:20–22

Notice that Job's reaction to death and destruction was to worship.

Later, after Satan caused Job to break out in painful boils, he said, "Though He slay me, yet will I trust Him" (Job 13:15).

King David faced the sickness of his infant son conceived from his sin with Bathsheba. Although the prophet Nathan told him that the child would die, David pleaded with God for his son's life by fasting and praying all night on the ground.

On the seventh day, when the baby died, David's servants were afraid to tell him, fearing that he might fall apart emotionally. Yet when David perceived from the servants' whispering that the child was gone, he "arose from the ground, washed and anointed himself, and changed his clothes; and he went into the house of the LORD and worshiped" (2 Samuel 12:20). Then he returned home and ate food. When his servants inquired as to this unexpected response, David replied:

> "While the child was alive, I fasted and wept; for I said, 'Who can tell whether the LORD will be gracious to me, that the child may live?' But now he is dead; why should I fast? Can I bring him back again? I shall go to him, but he shall not return to me."
>
> verses 22–23

Again, like Job, David's response was to worship.

As I said in chapter 6, let's choose not to be offended with God. Only in this life do we have the opportunity to react rightly to trials, tests, painful situations, and questions we cannot answer. When we live in glory, we will have no tests to pass or trials to weather. May our reaction now to infirmity and suffering be like that of Job and David. May we fall on our knees, pledge our allegiance to the Lord, and worship.

Persecution

Although this topic is not frequently covered in pulpits, we must grasp the revelation of responding rightly to suffering and outright persecution. Paul spoke about being content with much or little:

> I have learned in whatever state I am, to be content: I know how to be abased, and I know how to abound. Everywhere and in all things I have learned both to be full and to be hungry, both to abound and to suffer need. I can do all things through Christ who strengthens me.
>
> Philippians 4:11–13

One of my sisters was brought back from the brink of death by septicemia, blood poisoning. While in a state of near death, she began to have visions of suffering people. Some were flashbacks of suffering during World War II. She also saw people dying in a mudslide. Weeks after her experience, four people died in mudslides in western Canada. Another vision she had was of people dying while buried alive. A few months later, an apartment building in Florida collapsed, burying people alive. She saw other scenes of Jewish people being loaded onto buses and taken somewhere she knew was like a concentration camp. While she was having these visions, my sister sensed this main question: How do we respond rightly to suffering?

The suffering of believers in Jesus in the early Church and today is immense. The apostle Paul recounted being

> in labors more abundant, in stripes above measure, in prisons more frequently, in deaths often. From the Jews five times I received forty stripes minus one. Three times I was beaten

with rods; once I was stoned; three times I was shipwrecked;
a night and a day I have been in the deep; in journeys often,
in perils of waters, in perils of robbers, in perils of my own
countrymen, in perils of the Gentiles, in perils in the city, in
perils in the wilderness, in perils in the sea, in perils among
false brethren; in weariness and toil, in sleeplessness often, in
hunger and thirst, in fastings often, in cold and nakedness—
besides the other things, what comes upon me daily: my deep
concern for all the churches.

2 Corinthians 11:23–28

"If I must boast," Paul concluded, "I will boast in the things
which concern my infirmity" (verse 30). Yet Paul was also able
to say, at the end of his life, that knowing Jesus was worth it
all (see 2 Timothy 4:7–8).

Open Doors, a ministry to the persecuted, estimates that
around 365 million Christians are living in places where they experience high levels of persecution and discrimination. Between
fall 2022 and fall 2023, more than 4,998 Christians were killed
for their faith; 14,766 churches and other Christian properties
were attacked; 4,125 believers were detained without trial and arrested, sentenced, or imprisoned; 3,906 believers were abducted;
more than 3,200 Christians were raped, sexually harassed, or
forced to marry unbelievers; 42,849 were abused, physically or
mentally; and nearly 300,000 were forced to flee their homes—
more than double the number from the previous year.[2]

In North Korea being found out as a Christian is tanta-
mount to a death sentence. Believers are killed immediately
or deported to labor camps, where an estimated tens of thou-
sands are presently held.[3] In Nigeria more believers are killed
for their faith each year than everywhere else in the world

combined.[4] In Iran conversion from Islam to Christianity is illegal. Anyone caught is arrested and imprisoned and often subject to torture and abuse.[5]

China's surveillance system encroaches on her citizens and on the religious freedoms of Christians and other religious minorities. Facial-recognition cameras are present in most public places, including in churches to monitor worshipers.[6] Crosses on churches are torn down, house churches are raided, and leaders are imprisoned.[7]

Open Doors updates its World Watch List every year, naming the nations where Christians face the most extreme persecution and providing information on each country.[8] I use these details for prayer fodder, and lead prayer for the persecuted once a week.

Hebrews 13:3 reminds us, "Remember the prisoners as if chained with them—those who are mistreated—since you yourselves are in the body also." May we care for, pray for, give to, and otherwise inquire of the Lord as to how we can help the persecuted. May we cry out for the promises of Jesus:

"Blessed are those who are persecuted for righteousness' sake, for theirs is the kingdom of heaven. Blessed are you when they revile and persecute you, and say all kinds of evil against you falsely for My sake. Rejoice and be exceedingly glad, for great is your reward in heaven, for so they persecuted the prophets who were before you."

Matthew 5:10–12

Phoebe

Our fourth child was born at the crack of dawn on Christmas Day, a beautiful gift to our family. We named her Phoebe, meaning "bright shining one." An easy baby to raise, Phoebe was always smiling. Yet Phoebe changed after she received the measles, mumps, and rubella (MMR) vaccination at around eighteen months. She lost the ability to say words she had previously known, like *Dad, dog, run, car.* She no longer tracked us in her gaze and could no longer focus. She did not want to be held as much and instead became restless, energetic, and unable to discern danger.

John and I lost count of the doctors we visited. We said the same thing to all of them: "The vaccination caused this." Only two acknowledged that we could be right. No test gave a definitive diagnosis other than the catch-all phrase *global developmental delay* (GDD).

I understand that the connection is controversial. But the change in Phoebe to all of us in the family was marked. To say I was devastated would be an understatement. Many nights I lost sleep, asking myself, *Why did I let her have that needle?* I asked Phoebe over and over to forgive me. Agony filled my prayers, consumed with begging God for her healing and asking Him why He did not prevent this. I reminded Him that I had prayed every day over this precious child in my womb. *And I even work for You, God!*

Forgiving myself was a big first step. The guilt I was carrying was a burden that needed to be lifted. Then I needed to forgive—or a better way to say it would be, I needed to "release" God from my expectation that He should have intervened. God never does anything wrong, yet our perception of what He should or should not do leaves us with the need to let go of offense against Him.

A powerful encounter occurred when my friend Carol Arnott prayed over me one day at church. I was having difficulty knowing that I was now the mother of a special needs child. In the encounter, it was as if I were in the boat with the disciples in the windstorm, causing waves to beat against the boat and fill it with water (see Mark 4:35–41). I felt nauseous, sick with worry over Phoebe, and burdened with inner pain.

With authority, Carol declared, "Peace, be still."

The turmoil in my heart suddenly lifted. God met me in my state of weakness.

Sometime later I heard in my heart the loving voice of my heavenly Father: *Patricia, will you love Me anyway? Will you serve Me anyway? Will you get back up again and preach the goodness of God and pray for the sick anyway, even if your own child does not get healed?*

With tears streaming down my face, I replied, "Yes, Lord, where else can I go? You alone hold the words of life. I will love You, serve You, and trust You forever."

And so it is until this day. Phoebe is not entirely healed, although she graduated from a special program in high school, obtained a college certificate for culinary arts, works at a restaurant, and lives in a Christian community, where she bowls, swims, dances, and rides horses. She goes to church, dancing and flagging in the aisles; she loves Jesus; she reads her Bible; and she prays.

I look upon Phoebe as a Christmas Day gift to our family— a reminder that we all have special needs. We all need to be loved and to receive the revelation of the faithfulness of God. In our weakest moments He meets us, carries us, and lifts our burdens as we give them to Him.

I may not understand everything He allows to happen, but I believe in God's redemption, goodness, and never-ending love. I pledge my allegiance to Jesus. I will worship Him forever because He is worthy!

——————— PRAYER ———————

Lord, I may not understand all that happens in life, but I choose to trust You. Thank You for keeping me through times of trial. You are with me in the battle. Goodness and mercy will follow me all the days of my life.

10

FROM THIS LIFE TO THE NEXT

I have fought the good fight, I have finished the race, I have kept the faith. Finally, there is laid up for me the crown of righteousness, which the Lord, the righteous Judge, will give to me on that Day, and not to me only but also to all who have loved His appearing.

2 Timothy 4:7–8

Have you ever taken a trip to a foreign country after researching the specifics of the new land? You might purchase a travel book and learn about dining, climate, hotels, local modes of transportation, and the best sites to visit. Another future endeavor many are very intentional about is retirement. Planning for retirement can start years in advance with investments, retirement savings plans, pensions, employers' retirement plans, and possible moves.

In most cases vacations last a week or two, and retirement lasts years. Yet we put more time and effort into planning for both of these, compared with planning for where we will go after we die, which will last for eternity.

How does one prepare for life after life on earth? It is beneficial to investigate the numerous passages in the Book written by the Creator of humankind, of the universe, and of the afterlife. Knowing Him personally and surrendering to His Lordship in salvation is key. We will discuss this as we seek to live Revelation 19:7: "Let us be glad and rejoice and give Him glory, for the marriage of the Lamb has come, and His wife has made herself ready."

Beyond the Grave

Jesus spoke frequently about heaven, hell, and eternal life. He mentioned the word *heaven* (or some derivative) around 125 times in the New Testament. And of some 400 references in Scripture to hell, it was Jesus who spoke on it most. Why? Because He came to save us from ever having to go there. He gave messages of warning, which are messages of love.

The Gospel of Luke records a story Jesus told of a rich man and Lazarus. Lazarus was a beggar full of sores lying at the rich man's gate. When he died, he was carried by the angels to Abraham's bosom. The rich man also died and was in torment in Hades—the place of the dead.

The rich man asked Abraham to release Lazarus to give him a taste of water, "for I am tormented in this flame" (Luke 16:24). Abraham said that was not possible because of the "great gulf fixed" between them, "so that those who want to pass from here to you cannot, nor can those from there pass to us" (verse 26).

Then the rich man asked if Lazarus could be sent to his father's house to warn his five brothers of the reality of hell. But Abraham replied:

> "They have Moses and the prophets; let them hear them." And he said, "No, father Abraham; but if one goes to them from the dead, they will repent." But he said to him, "If they do not hear Moses and the prophets, neither will they be persuaded though one rise from the dead."
>
> verses 29–31

It is commonly thought that Jesus told this story as a parable. According to many scholars and commentaries, however, this was not a parable. First, no parable ever had a specific name in it, and this has two names: Abraham and Lazarus. Second, Jesus started the story by saying, "There was a certain rich man." And finally, Jesus quoted Abraham three times, stating twice that "Abraham said" (verses 25 and 29). If the patriarch Abraham had not said those things, Jesus would not have told the account as though he did.

It is clear to me, then, that this was not a parable. But regardless, it is instruction on hell from the mouth of the Lord Jesus. It confirms many other Scriptures of the reality of heaven and hell.

Hell is a place of suffering and torment where justice prevails, bringing inescapable exclusion from heaven. It also conveys the longing of those there (such as the rich man) to warn others to avoid this place.

Hell

In recent years some, even within the Church, have pushed to minimize or rewrite the reality of hell. The teachings of annihilationism (the cessation of existence after death, at least of the unsaved) and universalism (the salvation of all humankind, who will eventually live in heaven) are simply not biblical—yet many believe them, as they cannot reconcile a loving God with One who would allow everlasting punishment.

Scripture teaches us that "the everlasting fire [was] prepared for the devil and his angels" (Matthew 25:41), and that all who reject God and His provision to save us from our fallen, sinful state will be separated from Him eternally in what is known as hell. Here are a few of the Scriptures that speak of this reality: Deuteronomy 32:22; Job 15:30; 18:15–21; Psalm 9:17; 21:9; 49:19; Isaiah 14:9–11; 33:12–14; 34:8–10; 66:24; Ezekiel 31:14–17; 32:21; Daniel 12:2; Matthew 13:41–42; 18:8–9; Mark 9:43–48; Luke 13:24–28; 16:23–24; John 15:6; 2 Thessalonians 1:7–9; Jude 7; Revelation 14:10–11; 20:13–15; 21:8.

The great nineteenth-century preacher C. H. Spurgeon said:

> We speak of the wrath to come, and the everlasting punishment which God apportions to the impenitent, with fear and trembling; but we speak of it because we cannot escape from the conviction that it is taught in the word of God. . . . We must speak all the gospel, or else the blood of souls will stain our skirts at the last great day. However painful a duty it may be, it is none the less binding upon us.[1]

American revivalist preacher and theologian Jonathan Edwards said:

> It is an unreasonable and unscriptural notion of the mercy of God, that he is merciful in such a sense that he cannot bear that penal justice should be executed.[2]

From This Life to the Next

In short, God is merciful, kind, loving, and He is also holy and just.

Many years ago I heard the testimony of Bill Wiese, author of the *New York Times* bestseller *23 Minutes in Hell*. As a Christian real estate businessman, Bill had an out-of-body experience of being taken to hell for what felt to him like weeks. In reality it was 23 minutes. He describes hell in agonizing detail, details that align with many passages of Scripture that teach on the topic. Bill saw demonic beings that delight in torture; the pit of fire where screams of the burning ascend; the overwhelming terror that grips all who are there; the absence of any life, including water; and insatiable thirst.

After hearing Bill's testimony, I have not been the same. I was fueled with the compelling concern that those who do not know Jesus are headed for a Christless eternity, and with greater fervor to pray for the lost and to take action to win souls. I recommend Bill's online teachings and books.[3]

Heaven

In the Upper Room Discourse, after celebrating the Passover, Jesus spoke to His disciples about what is to come (see John 13–17). He was to go to the cross the next day, so He was preparing them—and us—for life with God.

Jesus told His disciples that, although He was leaving them, He would go before them:

> "Let not your heart be troubled; you believe in God, believe also in Me. In My Father's house are many mansions [dwelling places]; if it were not so, I would have told you. I go to prepare

151

a place for you. And if I go and prepare a place for you, I will come again and receive you to Myself; that where I am, there you may be also."

John 14:1–3

In the first chapter of this book, I observed that Jesus used wedding language in this passage from John 14 (as He did in other places as well). I explained that, in Jewish tradition at the time, a bridegroom would make his intentions known to the father and family of the prospective bride. There followed a betrothal covenant, in which the bridegroom left gifts with the family to pledge his return for his bride. Then he would build a bridal chamber in his father's house. Only after the inspection of this chamber by the father would the son be released to go and get his bride.

At the Last Supper, the night before He was crucified, the disciples would have understood the bridal imagery Jesus was using, yet they did not know how it pertained to Jesus or to them.

Thomas said to Him, "Lord, we do not know where You are going, and how can we know the way?"

Jesus said to him, "I am the way, the truth, and the life. No one comes to the Father except through Me."

John 14:5–6

It is easier for us, given the rest of the New Testament, to understand the bridal imagery Jesus was using. We know that the Church is His Bride, and that He is coming back for us. Either we go to Him, or the day comes when He will come on the clouds for us. Every eye will see Him, every tongue will confess, and every knee will bow. In the meantime, He is preparing a place for us in what is known as heaven.

In the Bible the word *heaven* is plural, *heavens*, rather than singular, in some 168 references, such as Hebrews 1:10: "You, Lord, in the beginning laid the foundation of the earth, and the heavens are the work of Your hands."

The Scriptures refer to the first heaven as the realm of human existence—what we see with our natural eyes. The second heaven is commonly thought of as the realm where Satan rules his evil empire with demons and fallen angels—what Ephesians 6:12 calls "spiritual hosts of wickedness in the heavenly places." The third heaven, mentioned in 2 Corinthians 12:2, speaks of paradise, where God rules and reigns over the universe with His holy angels, and where Jesus is "seated . . . at His right hand" (Ephesians 1:20).

The word *heavens* is generally plural rather than singular, I believe, because we read of various places located in what we know as heaven. There is, for example, the throne where God sits (see Revelation 4); the place of judgment, where books will be opened, including "the Book of Life" (Revelation 20:12, 15); "a pure river of water of life" and "the tree of life" (Revelation 22:1–2); meadows, flowers, and green pastures (see Psalm 23).

"The holy city, New Jerusalem, coming down out of heaven from God" (Revelation 21:2) will descend in the age to come. It is a cube 1,380 miles high, wide, and long. Each of its twelve gates is a single pearl, and its walls are 216 feet thick. The streets of New Jerusalem are pure gold, like transparent glass. The last verse of Revelation 21 says, "There shall by no means enter it anything that defiles, or causes an abomination or a lie, but only those who are written in the Lamb's Book of Life."

Heaven is a real place. We have the honor of being invited to live there someday, because of the One who died in our place, rose from the dead, lives forevermore, and who will come again to bring us to Himself.

Near-Death Experiences

At times the Lord has allowed some to go beyond the veil of death and return to tell about it. An estimated nine million people have undergone a near-death experience (NDE). Probably not all are authentic, but most cannot be discounted as figments of imagination, especially from people with medical proof of having been clinically dead.

One factor to recognize is the difference between what people report experiencing and the interpretation they give to what they experienced. NDEs have happened to Christians and non-Christians across the globe from various religions, ages, and socioeconomic backgrounds.

I highly recommend a book called *Imagine Heaven* by John Burke. Formerly an engineer, Burke began to read or hear near-death stories, nearly a thousand in all, in which he saw notable commonalities. His *New York Times* bestseller, written since he became a pastor, recounts more than a hundred stories of people who had been clinically dead or near death and who came back with amazing stories to tell.

Burke identifies numerous lessons from those who have gone beyond and returned. They received a revelation of God's love for them; they now wanted to become people of love; and they experienced a powerful new desire to read the Bible, pray, and know God.[4]

Let's explore the experiences of some who have gone beyond the veil and then returned.

Pleading in the Smoke

Ron Reagan was a young man making terrible choices in life. One day, after getting into a fight in a store, his arm was cut open by a broken bottle, severing a muscle and several arteries. On his way to the hospital, as he was losing consciousness, he began to leave his body. In his own words:

> The ambulance looked like it had exploded, like it had blown up. Suddenly I was moving through a tunnel. And after some time, coming out of the smoke, out of the darkness, I began to hear the voices of a multitude of people, screaming and groaning and crying. As I looked down, the sensation was looking down upon a volcanic opening, and seeing fire and smoke and people inside of this burning place, screaming and crying. They were burning, but they weren't burning up; they weren't being consumed. . . .
>
> I began to recognize many of the people I was seeing in these flames, as if a close-up lens on a camera was bringing their faces close to me. I could see their features. I could see the agony and pain and frustration. And a number of them began to call my name, saying, "Ronnie, don't come to this place. There's no way out, there's no escape." . . . The smell was like sulfur, like an electric welder, and the stench was terrible.[5]

Reagan survived the attack, and his arm was spared with almost a hundred stitches. But he could not get the experience out of his mind. It scared him to death, although he turned to drugs and alcohol for relief. Several months later he accepted Jesus as Lord and Savior, and his life was transformed.

The Way of Love

Steve Sjogren was a prominent church pastor doing good work in his city. After suffering a heart attack, while doctors were trying to revive him, he "hovered" on the room's ceiling while God spoke to him in a voice "like a hundred friends talking in harmonious unison." Sjogren recounts that God communicated an important message that would influence his perspective and mission into the future:

> We did not communicate just with words, but also with memories and images. God let me know how much He valued me. It's almost impossible to describe the perfect sense of acceptance that surrounded me, yet even in the midst of this very personal embrace, part of me knew that not everything in my life had matched what God had intended for me. . . .
>
> The doctors were in emergency mode, and God was calmly quizzing me. "Do you know the names of your children's friends?" He asked. This was not a daydream. God wanted to know the answer, but I couldn't list a single one! . . .
>
> The realization struck me like a bolt of lightning. I hadn't taken the time to get to know my children's best friends and long-term buddies. . . . These friends often visited our house. They were always welcome, but I was anything but hospitable. When they came, I was usually fixated on one project or another. Many times, I just wasn't there.[6]

During this NDE, the Lord redirected Steve Sjogren deeper into the way of love.

A Changed Life

Ian McCormack tells his story in his book *Night Dive to Heaven*.[7] Before his near-death experience, he was a self-described 26-year-old atheist on a two-year world tour of self-discovery. He had traveled from his native New Zealand to Mauritius, an island country in the Indian Ocean, living a "free spirit" lifestyle of multiple relationships, drugs, and surfing.

One evening as he was diving for lobsters, he was stung by five box jellyfish. The sting of just one can be deadly in minutes. In the ambulance, as paralysis started to take over his body, Ian knew he was dying. But he saw a vision of his mother, a Christian, praying for him, and remembered her saying that Jesus would hear and forgive him if he called out to Him. So he began to cry out to God, trying to remember a prayer his mother had taught him as a boy.

He started to pray the Lord's Prayer as its words appeared in his field of vision: "Your Kingdom come, Your will be done." He knew he had been doing everything *but* God's will. Then the faces of people who had wronged him flashed before his eyes, and he knew God was saying to forgive them, which he tried to do.

At the hospital the doctors could not save his life. A death certificate was signed, and his body removed to another part of the hospital.

Meanwhile, Ian found himself in a dark place. His hand, when he tried to touch his face, went right through it. Fear and dread filled him. He knew he was in hell. Again he cried out to God for help.

Suddenly a brilliant beam of light broke through, and he rose upward through a tunnel, where he found himself in the presence of incredible light and power. Waves of divine love washed over him as he realized he was standing before the God he had never believed in. His fear of judgment washed away, and he wept in the presence of indescribable light and love.

A voice spoke to him, which he knew was Jesus, asking him to choose to stay in heaven or return to earth. He wanted to stay. But once again he saw his mother praying for him, and he realized she would assume he had died without faith. For her sake, so she would know her prayers had been answered, he asked to be returned to earth. He also saw a vision of family members, friends, and then a sea of unknown faces—all who needed to know the truth about heaven and hell and to accept Jesus as Savior and Lord.

The next moment Ian awoke in the hospital. He had been clinically dead for fifteen minutes. A woman attending to his body screamed as he returned to life.

The trajectory of Ian's life changed. He became a pastor and evangelist and has traveled the world telling his miraculous story.

The Terror of Hell

Cardiologist Maurice Rawlings did not believe in God or the afterlife—until one of his patients suffered cardiac arrest during a stress test and dropped dead onto the floor. A nurse began cardiopulmonary resuscitation while Rawlings did external heart massage, trying to restore a steady heartbeat. He tells the story of the crisis:

> The patient began "coming to." But whenever I would reach for instruments or otherwise interrupt my compression of his chest, the patient would again lose consciousness . . . and die once more. Each time he regained heartbeat and respiration, the patient screamed, "I am in hell!" He was terrified and pleaded with me to help him. I was scared to death. In fact, this episode *literally* scared the hell out of me! . . . He said, "Don't you understand? I am in hell. Each time you quit I go back to hell! Don't let me go back to hell!" . . .
>
> I dismissed his complaint and told him to keep his "hell" to himself. . . . But the man was serious. . . . After several death

episodes he finally asked me, "How do I stay out of hell? . . . I don't know how. Pray for me."

Pray for him! *What nerve!* I told him I was a doctor, not a preacher.

"Pray for me!" he repeated.[8]

So as Rawlings continued working on the patient's heart, he called on his Sunday school days and had the man repeat a patchwork prayer:

Lord Jesus, I ask You to keep me out of hell. Forgive my sins. I turn my life over to you. If I die, I want to go to heaven. If I live, I'll be "on the hook" forever.

The patient's heartbeat stabilized, and Dr. Rawlings visited him a few days later. But when he asked his patient what he had seen in hell, the man could recall none of it—only pleasant things he had seen after asking Jesus for forgiveness.

Maurice Rawlings became a Christian, began to study near-death experiences, wrote books, and became a voice in the medical community for the importance of the spiritual element in the lives of patients.[9]

Jesus Saves

Howard Storm was a self-described narcissistic atheist who did not believe in the afterlife, but that "the one who dies with the most toys wins."[10] He was teaching art at a Kentucky university when he and his wife led students on a field trip to Paris. There he developed a deadly bowel perforation and, while awaiting emergency surgery, passed into the next life.

Initially Storm was dragged into realms of darkness, fear, and horror, where cruel beings tortured him. Then he thought of praying. In desperation, although he did not even believe in God, he patched together a prayer based on parts of the Twenty-Third Psalm, "The Star-Spangled Banner," the Lord's Prayer, the Pledge of Allegiance, and "God Bless America."

Amazingly, as he prayed his jumbled prayer, the cruel beings torturing him began to rage and back off—as if, he thought, he were throwing boiling oil on them. Then, with nothing to lose, Howard yelled into the darkness, "Jesus, save me!"

Far in the distance, he saw a pinpoint of brilliant, beautiful light, which came closer and closer until Jesus Christ appeared to him. The Man he had never believed in hugged him as he wept. Repenting of his unbelief and reveling in the love of God, Howard Storm was sent back to earth. He ended up leaving his university post to attend seminary and become a pastor.

Life Review

For some a near-death experience is accompanied by an overview of one's life in flashes of incidents, like watching a fast-moving movie screen or reexperiencing one's life in a 3-D panoramic replay. Not only actions but also motives are revealed, and how these have affected others. This life review may take place in God's presence as He gently guides the person to see what matters most and what will last forever.

Most life reviews start with a question from God, spoken not in judgment but in love, to prompt learning and reflection.

Howard Storm, the art professor who patched together a prayer and cried out to Jesus to save him, described the life review he experienced, which was directed by Jesus and angels in a semicircle around him:

> The scenes they showed me were often of incidents I had forgotten. They showed their effects on people's lives, of which I had no previous knowledge. . . . They showed me scenes from my life that I would not have chosen, and they eliminated scenes from my life that I wanted them to see. . . .
>
> The angels showed me how my father's compulsion to be successful was driving him toward increasing impatience and rage with his family. I saw how my mother, sisters, and I each developed different means of coping with his unpredictable mood swings. . . .
>
> It was horrifying to see how I had become so much like my father, putting status and success above everything else. I believed that my worth was measured by my success in my chosen career. . . . When the angels showed me how destructive this was to the well-being of my loved ones, I wanted to end my life review. They insisted that I needed to see the truth of my life and learn from it. . . .
>
> How many people will cry out to Jesus Christ when they die and be given a life review? He will say to them, "You called me but I never knew you. When did you show compassion to your brother or sister? When did you love me?"[11]

Howard Storm's life was transformed as a result.

Storm and others with near-death experiences and life reviews come back with clarity on two things: that God is love, and that how we love each other matters deeply to God. John Burke states:

> I'm afraid there will be too many Christians from our generation who felt really good about what they believed and

being moral (and yes, that matters), but they thought they were better than others and were not kind or loving to those who struggled in ways they didn't, and I think this life review is going to be a shocker. Jesus told us what mattered most to him, but sometimes we lose sight of its priority.[12]

We observed in chapter 1 that Jesus reduced all the commandments in the Law to two:

> "'You shall love the LORD your God with all your heart, with all your soul, and with all your mind.' This is the first and great commandment. And the second is like it: 'You shall love your neighbor as yourself.'"
>
> Matthew 22:37–39

How are we doing at the two most important things Jesus said we would ever do?

Eternal Rewards

Caesarea Maritima is an ancient port on the Mediterranean Sea where the apostle Paul was imprisoned for a time. Today you can still see the ruins of the hippodrome where athletes trained for the Actian Games (modeled after the Greek Olympics). From Paul's prison window he could see them prepare. He wrote in 1 Corinthians 9:24–27:

> Do you not know that those who run in a race all run, but one receives the prize? Run in such a way that you may obtain it. . . . Now they do it to obtain a perishable crown, but we for an imperishable crown. Therefore I run thus: not with

uncertainty. Thus I fight: not as one who beats the air. But I discipline my body and bring it into subjection.

Paul viewed the incredible discipline the athletes exercised, training for a temporal prize. How much more important for believers to discipline themselves to prepare for eternity and eternal rewards?

We get to heaven because of what Jesus did on the cross. Yet the Bible says there are rewards in heaven for how we live our lives here on earth. Jesus said that "whoever gives one of these little ones only a cup of cold water" receives a reward (Matthew 10:42). Crowns are also cited in Scriptures such as James 1:12, which says that the one who endures temptation "will receive the crown of life which the Lord has promised to those who love Him."

The opportunity to reign with Jesus in the millennial Kingdom is recorded in passages such as 1 Corinthians 6:2–3 (the saints will judge the world) and the parable of minas (talents) of Luke 19:12–26: "And [the master] said to him, 'Well done, good servant; because you were faithful in a very little, have authority over ten cities" (verse 17).

First Peter 1:4–5 speaks of

an inheritance incorruptible and undefiled and that does not fade away, reserved in heaven for you, who are kept by the power of God through faith for salvation ready to be revealed in the last time.

And Paul, preparing to depart from this world, shared:

I have fought the good fight, I have finished the race, I have kept the faith. Finally, there is laid up for me the crown of righteousness, which the Lord, the righteous Judge, will give to me on that Day, and not to me only but also to all who have loved His appearing.

2 Timothy 4:7–8

Treasures in Heaven

James Dobson, founder of the ministry Focus on the Family, described his longing to be the best tennis player on his college campus. He made that goal and received a coveted trophy for his accomplishment. It was displayed with pride in a glass case at the college. Thirty years later Dobson received a package from a friend who had attended the same school. It was the trophy, dusty and scratched, that Dobson had worked hard to acquire. The friend had found it in a dumpster.[13]

It is easy to see the contrast between Dobson's sought-after trophy, destined for the trash, and the eternal treasures Jesus spoke of:

"Do not lay up for yourselves treasures on earth, where moth and rust destroy and where thieves break in and steal; but lay up for yourselves treasures in heaven, where neither moth nor rust destroys and where thieves do not break in and steal. For where your treasure is, there your heart will be also."

Matthew 6:19–21

Billy Graham also wrote of heavenly treasures:

Five minutes after I'm in heaven . . . suddenly the things I thought important—tomorrow's tasks, the plans for the dinner at my church, my success or failure in pleasing those around me—these will matter not at all. And the things to which I gave but little thought—the word about Christ to the man next door, the moment (how short it was) of earnest prayer for the Lord's work in far-off lands, the confessing and forsaking of that secret sin—will stand as real and enduring. Five minutes after I'm in heaven I'll be overwhelmed by the truths I've known but somehow never grasped. I'll realize then that it's what I am in Christ that comes first with God.[14]

The lives we live on earth are short compared to eternity. Our seventy, eighty, or even ninety years are but a moment compared to forever and ever in the next life. Yet how we live our lives here on earth affects eternity significantly. And heaven and hell, as we have seen, are real.

Learning to think eternally helps us live well in this life. When we are tempted to be offended, to say something unkind, or to walk away from God's ways, it will help us to remember eternity.

Napoleon Bonaparte, one of the most successful military leaders in history, is reported to have said:

Alexander, Caesar, Charlemagne, and myself have founded empires. But on what did we rest the creations of our genius? Upon *force*! Jesus Christ alone founded his empire upon love; and at this moment millions of men would die for him.[15]

Decision for Eternity

The book of Romans outlines the way of salvation in passages sometimes referred to as the Romans Road:

1. God is a holy, perfect God, and we all have sinned. Thus there is a gap between God and us. Romans 3:23: "All have sinned and fall short of the glory of God."

2. We deserve death, which was the price to bridge the gap between a holy God and us. Romans 6:23: "The wages of sin is death, but the gift of God is eternal life in Christ Jesus our Lord."

3. Jesus, the Son of God, stepped out of heaven to come to earth as a baby in the womb of a virgin, to be born in a manger, and to die on a cruel cross, to pay the price of death that we owed for our sins. Romans 5:8: "God demonstrates His own love toward us, in that while we were still sinners, Christ died for us."

4. To come into right standing before God, all we do is confess and believe that Jesus died for us and receive Him as Lord and Savior. Romans 10:9–10: "If you confess with your mouth the Lord Jesus and believe in your heart that God has raised Him from the dead, you will be saved. For with the heart one believes unto righteousness, and with the mouth confession is made unto salvation." Romans 10:13: "Whoever calls on the name of the LORD shall be saved."

5. We can live in peace and victory through faith in Jesus; and live with Him and the Father forever in heavenly glory after this life. Romans 5:1–2: "Having been justified by faith, we have peace with God through our Lord Jesus Christ, through whom also we have access by faith into this grace in which we stand, and rejoice in hope of the glory of God."

Life is full of a myriad of choices—from what we will say at any given moment, to the relationships we foster, to the thoughts we allow to fill our minds. By far the most crucial decision we will ever make—even more important than whom we marry or the career path we follow—is the decision to accept Jesus Christ as Savior and Lord. This decision not only guides our lives on earth; it is of eternal consequence.

Please trust the truth contained in the Bible and the witness of millions of believers from times past and present. Prepare for Jesus' return and your eternity. Choose Jesus. Choose life.

Surrender

The white flag during war, accompanied by the surrender of soldiers, is seen as an act of defeat. Yet in the spiritual sense, throwing up the white flag of surrender to Jesus is an act of victory.

Please pray this:

Lord Jesus, today I choose to surrender to You. Be Lord of my life. Today I accept Your will and Your way. Forgive me for living my own will and my own way, and for the sins I have committed. Help me to know You and live the life You have designed for me. I say yes to You. I dedicate the rest of my life to You. I receive Your love; I receive You as Savior; I receive Your leading. I surrender.

What now? Simply go and fall in love. Receive and believe in the God of love who has pursued you all your life. All you are doing now is turning to face Him and receive His embrace.

Talk to Him just as you would talk to a person. The exercise of prayer is a way of connection. He hears, and He often talks back in words of love and kindness to your spirit.

And read the Bible. Start with the Gospel of John and just keep reading day after day. The Bible is God's manual for living.

Get involved in a life-giving church that will surround you with people who will help strengthen your resolve to walk on a new path.

When the last trumpet sounds, every knee will bow and all of us will see the Lord Jesus Christ face-to-face. Then every tongue will confess Jesus as Lord. But we get to do that willingly now, out of love and choice. When we do, we will be ready for that day when He splits the sky. Prepare for His return and your eternity. He will be worth it all!

——————————— PRAYER ———————————

Lord, thank You for helping me live with the revelation of eternity. Help me learn to love in every area of my life. Help me get ready for the day I meet You face-to-face and live with You for eternity.

NOTES

Chapter 1 From Lukewarmness to Wholeheartedness

1. "Direction in Dilemma" (sermon), November 22, 1863, Metropolitan Tabernacle, Newington, London, in *Spurgeon's Sermons*, vol. 9, Christian Classics Ethereal Library, accessed July 1, 2024, https://ccel.org/ccel/spurgeon/sermons09/sermons09.lv.html.

Chapter 2 From Living without Margins to Sabbath Rest

1. C. S. Lewis, *The Problem of Pain* (New York: HarperOne, 2001), 91.

2. Bob Jones, "The 100-Year Prophecy (2020–2029): A Decade of Rest," YouTube video posted by Prophetic Watch, 2:37, September 29, 2020, https://www.youtube.com/watch?v=_ZVdop1q3SE.

3. Rebecca Ahrnsbrak and Marie N. Stagnitti, "Comparison of Antidepressant and Antipsychotic Utilization and Expenditures in the U.S. Civilian Noninstitutionalized Population, 2013 and 2018," February 2021, Agency for Healthcare Research and Quality, https://meps.ahrq.gov/data_files/publications/st534/stat534.shtml.

4. "Facts about Suicide," U.S. Centers for Disease Control and Prevention, April 25, 2024, https://www.cdc.gov/suicide/facts/index.html.

5. Jessica Booth, "Anxiety Statistics and Facts," Health, *Forbes*, October 23, 2023, https://www.forbes.com/health/mind/anxiety-statistics.

6. Staff writer, "Your Mental Health: Younger People More Anxious; Stress Addiction a Growing Concern," *Bartlesville Examiner-Enterprise*, February 5, 2014, https://www.examiner-enterprise.com/story/lifestyle/2014/02/05/your-mental-health-younger-people/27387997007.

7. "Panic Attacks & Panic Disorder," Cleveland Clinic, last reviewed February 12, 2023, https://my.clevelandclinic.org/health/diseases/4451-panic-attack-panic-disorder.

8. Shayna Waltower, "50-Hour Workweeks? How to Cut Back on the New Normal," *Business News Daily*, October 24, 2023, https://www.businessnewsdaily.com/8357-longer-work-weeks.html.

9. Kabir Sehgal and Deepak Chopra, "Stanford Professor: Working This Many Hours a Week Is Basically Pointless," Make It, CNBC, March 20, 2019, https://www.cnbc.com/2019/03/20/stanford-study-longer-hours-doesnt-make-you-more-productive-heres-how-to-get-more-done-by-doing-less.html.

10. John Mark Comer, *The Ruthless Elimination of Hurry* (Colorado Springs: WaterBrook, 2019), 19.

11. *The Social Dilemma*, directed by Jeff Orlowski, written by Davis Coombe, Vickie Curtis, Jeff Orlowski, Netflix, September 9, 2020.

12. Tim Bajarin, "Spending Time on Social Media Is Both Good and Bad," *Forbes*, September 19, 2023, https://www.forbes.com/sites/timbajarin/2023/09/19/spending-time-on-social-media-is-both-good-and-bad.

13. Eric Andrew-Gee, "Your Smartphone Is Making You Stupid, Antisocial and Unhealthy," *The Globe and Mail*, December 15, 2022, https://www.theglobeandmail.com/technology/your-smartphone-is-making-you-stupid/article37511900/.

14. Comer, *Ruthless Elimination of Hurry*, 71.

15. Walter Brueggemann, *Sabbath as Resistance* (Louisville: Westminster John Knox, 2017), xiv.

16. Orthodox Union staff, "The 39 Categories of Sabbath Work Prohibited by Law," Orthodox Union, July 17, 2006, https://www.ou.org/holidays/the_thirty_nine_categories_of_sabbath_work_prohibited_by_law.

17. "Happiness and Life Satisfaction: A Look at Data by Division," Office of Archives, Statistics, and Research, General Conference of Seventh-day Adventists, February 15, 2023, https://www.adventistresearch.info/happiness-and-life-satisfaction-a-look-at-data-by-division.

18. Ryan Buxton, "What Seventh-Day Adventists Get Right That Lengthens Their Life Expectancy," HuffPost, July 31, 2014, https://www.huffpost.com/entry/seventh-day-adventists-life-expectancy_n_5638098.

19. Daniel Kahneman and Angus Deaton, "High Income Improves Evaluation of Life but Not Emotional Well-Being," Proceedings of the National Academy of Sciences of the United States of America, September 7, 2010, https://www.pnas.org/doi/10.1073/pnas.1011492107.

20. "Profile: Hobby Lobby Stores," *Forbes*, accessed June 29, 2024, https://www.forbes.com/companies/hobby-lobby-stores.

21. "Leading Quick Service Restaurant (QSR) Chains in the United States in 2022, by Sales per Unit," Statista, November 16, 2023, https://www.statista.com/statistics/242870/average-sales-per-system-unit-of-quick-service-restaurant-chains.

Chapter 3 From Ingratitude to the Power of Thankfulness

1. MindValley Academy, "The Health Benefits of Gratitude," *Conscious Lifestyle*, accessed July 1, 2024, https://www.consciouslifestylemag.com/benefits-of-gratitude-research.

2. Ibid.

3. Kyle Benson, "The #1 Thing Couples Fight About," The Gottman Institute, August 9, 2016, https://www.gottman.com/blog/one-thing-couples-fight-about/.

4. Sarah Ban Breathnach, *Simple Abundance: 365 Days to a Balanced and Joyful Life* (New York: Grand Central Publishing, 2019), 365.

Chapter 4 From Brokenness to Communion

1. Christie Eisner, *Finding the Afikomen: Encountering Jesus in the Spring Feasts* (Amazon, 2015), 175–176.

2. Ann Voskamp, *One Thousand Gifts Devotional: Reflections on Finding Everyday Graces* (Nashville: W Publishing, 2012), 161; Ann Voskamp, *One Thousand Gifts: A Dare to Live Fully, Right Where You Are* (Grand Rapids: Zondervan, 2010), 58, 57.

3. Voskamp, *One Thousand Gifts*, 135.

4. Beni Johnson with Bill Johnson, *The Power of Communion* (Shippensburg, PA: Destiny Image, 2019), 149.

5. Ibid., 22.

6. Ibid., 159.

7. Ibid., 139.

Chapter 5 From Pride to Humility

1. "Captain Sir Arthur H. Rostron, K.B.E., R.D., R.N.R.," Gjenvick-Gjønvik Archives, accessed July 1, 2024, https://www.ggarchives.com/Ocean Travel/SteamshipCaptains/CaptainArthurHRostron.html.

2. Usually attributed to Andrew Murray, although the precise work of his where it originally appeared is unknown.

Chapter 6 From Offense to Freedom

1. "The U.S. Lawsuit System Costs America's Small Businesses $160 Billion," U.S. Chamber of Commerce Institute for Legal Reform, January 4, 2024, https://instituteforlegalreform.com/blog/the-us-lawsuit-system-costs-americas-small-businesses-160-billion.

2. Christine Ro, "The Truth about Family Estrangement," BBC, March 31, 2019, https://www.bbc.com/future/article/20190328-family-estrangement-causes.

3. Emanuella Grinberg and Carma Hassan, "University of Louisville President Sorry for Photo of Staff in Ponchos, Sombreros," CNN, October

31, 2015, https://www.cnn.com/2015/10/31/living/university-louisville
-racist-staff-party-feat/index.html.

4. "Yale Teacher Resigns over Halloween Costume Controversy," CBS
News, December 7, 2015, https://www.cbsnews.com/news/yale-teacher
-resigns-over-halloween-costume-controversy.

5. "The Woke Agenda and Its Influence on Churches and Colleges," Paul
Chappell, March 29, 2023, https://paulchappell.com/2023/03/29/the-woke
-agenda-and-its-influence.

6. Jack W. Hayford, exec. ed., *NKJV Spirit-Filled Life Bible*, 3rd ed. (Nashville: Thomas Nelson, 2018), 1385.

7. John Bevere, *The Bait of Satan: Living Free from the Deadly Trap of Offense*, 20th anniversary ed. (Lake Mary, FL: Charisma, 2014), 68.

8. Kathy DeGraw, "How to Identify the Spirit of Offense and Move
Toward Healing," *Charisma*, November 5, 2015, https://mycharisma.com
/spiritled-living/purposeidentity/how-to-identify-the-spirit-of-offense-and
-move-toward-healing.

9. Voice of the Martyrs made a movie of Sabina's life called *Sabina: Tortured for Christ*. See https://www.sabinamovie.com/online.

10. A. W. Tozer, *My Daily Pursuit: Devotions for Every Day* (Minneapolis:
Bethany House, 2014), 50.

11. Quoted by Burk Parsons, "A Sower Went Out to Sow," Ligonier
Ministries, June 1, 2009, https://www.ligonier.org/learn/articles/sower-went
-out-sow.

12. Sam Harris, interview with Chris Anderson, "Making Sense with
Sam Harris," The TED Interview, Podgist, October 30, 2018, https://www
.podgist.com/making-sense-sam-harris/the-ted-interview/index.html.

Chapter 7 From Bitterness to Forgiveness

1. John M. Perkins, *One Blood: Parting Words to the Church on Race and
Love* (Chicago: Moody, 2018), 99.

2. Corrie ten Boom, "Guideposts Classics: Corrie ten Boom on Forgiveness," *Guideposts*, November 1972, https://guideposts.org/positive-living
/guideposts-classics-corrie-ten-boom-forgiveness.

3. Corrie ten Boom, *Amazing Love* (Fort Washington, PA: Christian Lit-
erature Crusade, 1953), 10–12.

Chapter 8 From Orphan Heart to Sonship

1. "Fact Sheet: Fathers Matter—Pass It On," America First Policy Institute, May 30, 2023, https://americafirstpolicy.com/issues/fact-sheet-fathers
-matter-pass-it-on.

2. Ray Williams, "The Decline of Fatherhood and the Male Identity Crisis," Father Matters, accessed June 25, 2024, https://fathermatters.org/the
-decline-of-fatherhood-and-the-male-identity-crisis.

3. Bessel van der Kolk, *The Body Keeps the Score: Brain, Mind, and Body in the Healing of Trauma* (New York: Penguin, 2015), 133–135.

4. Adapted with permission, Jack and Trisha Frost, "From Orphan to Sonship," Shiloh Place Ministries, accessed July 1, 2024, https://irp-cdn.multiscreensite.com/89f1fea9/files/uploaded/Orphan-Son-Chart_lrOkS9RiqSXWVl4pvwky.pdf.

Chapter 9 From Trials to Triumph

1. Kathryn Kuhlman, *God Can Do It Again* (Old Tappan, NJ: Revell, 1974), 250–255.

2. "13 Christians a Day Killed for Their Faith," Open Doors US, January 30, 2024, https://www.opendoorsus.org/en-US/stories/13-christians-killed-day-average; and "Trends," Open Doors US, accessed June 25, 2024, https://www.opendoorsus.org/en-US/persecution/persecution-trends.

3. "What Does Persecution Look Like in North Korea?," Open Doors US, accessed June 25, 2024, https://www.opendoorsus.org/en-US/persecution/countries/north-korea.

4. "What Does Persecution Look Like in Nigeria?," Open Doors US, accessed June 25, 2024, https://www.opendoorsus.org/en-US/persecution/countries/nigeria.

5. "What Does Persecution Look Like in Iran?," accessed June 25, 2024, https://www.opendoorsus.org/en-US/persecution/countries/iran.

6. Rebecca Paveley, "Chinese Christians Face Increasing Surveillance and Repression," *Church Times*, February 16, 2024, https://www.churchtimes.co.uk/articles/2024/16-february/news/world/chinese-christians-face-increasing-surveillance-and-repression-say-analysts.

7. "China's War on Faith," NC Family Policy Council, March 4, 2022, https://www.ncfamily.org/china-war-on-faith.

8. "World Watch List 2024," Open Doors US, accessed June 25, 2024, https://www.opendoors.org/en-US/persecution/countries.

Chapter 10 From This Life to the Next

1. Charles Haddon Spurgeon, "A Private Enquiry" (sermon), January 18, 1891, The Spurgeon Center, accessed June 14, 2024, https://www.spurgeon.org/resource-library/sermons/a-private-enquiry.

2. Jonathan Edwards, "The Eternity of Hell's Torments" (sermon), April 1739, Bible Bulletin Board, accessed July 22, 2024, https://www.biblebb.com/files/edwards/eternity.htm.

3. Bill Wiese, "The Man Who Went to Hell," January 16, 2013, https://www.youtube.com/watch?v=AYxKRoONrfY.

4. John Burke, *Imagine Heaven* (Grand Rapids: Baker Books, 2015), 246–248.

5. Maurice Rawlings, "To Hell and Back," January 13, 2011, https://www.youtube.com/watch?v=Z6RoO6rK5aw.

6. Steve Sjogren, *The Day I Died: An Unforgettable Story of Life after Death* (Minneapolis: Bethany House, 2006), 30, 94.

7. Ian McCormack, *Night Dive to Heaven* (Winter Springs, FL: EABooks, 2023).

8. Maurice Rawlings, *Beyond Death's Door* (Nashville: Thomas Nelson, 1978), 18–20.

9. Maurice Rawlings, "It Literally Scared the Hell Out of Me," Freedom Church, January 4, 2019, https://www.youtube.com/watch?v=8x9EeoGqGC4.

10. Howard Storm, *My Descent into Death: A Second Chance at Life* (New York: Doubleday, 2005), 23.

11. Ibid., 30, 32, 34, 35–37.

12. John Burke, "What's after Life?," Gateway Church Austin, May 3, 2020, https://www.ericbryant.org/2020/05/03/whats-after-life-the-life-review-with-john-burke/.

13. Huntington University, "Dobson to Graduates: 'Be There,'" May 22, 1997, news release, https://www.huntington.edu/news/dobson-to-graduates-be-there.

14. Billy Graham, *Death and the Life After* (Nashville: Thomas Nelson, 2011), 17.

15. John S. C. Abbott, *The History of Napoleon Bonaparte*, vol. 1 (New York: Harper and Brothers, 1855), 246.

PATRICIA BOOTSMA is a lover of Jesus who grew up on a Canadian farm, riding horses, milking cows, and praying regularly for the Jewish people, as she heard the stories of her parents, who grew up in the Netherlands under Nazi occupation.

Patricia met and married John Bootsma in the Stratford, Ontario, church they attended, pastored by John and Carol Arnott. They followed the Arnotts to Toronto, becoming pastors with them in what became Catch the Fire Toronto and a move of God known as the Toronto Blessing, which made an impact around the world. John and Patricia are still pastors with Catch the Fire and are now located in Kansas City, Missouri, where they pastor CTF KC.

Patricia has started and led houses of prayer for many years, and is the global prayer leader for JH Israel, leading daily prayer for Israel and the Israel Virtual House of Prayer, an online community of prayer with participants from 28 nations. She has also authored four books, including *Raising Burning Hearts: Parenting and Mentoring Next Generation Lovers of God*.

John and Patricia take great delight in their six children, four of whom are married, and nine grandchildren, all of whom love Jesus passionately. John and Patricia play pickleball, work out in the Jewish Community Center of Kansas City gym, and cheer on the Kansas City Chiefs.

CONNECT WITH PATRICIA:

PatriciaBootsma.com

/BootsmaPatricia

@BootsmaPatricia